SPEECH
SIMPLIFIED

HOW TO CAPTIVATE YOUR AUDIENCE

Dr. Mohsen al Attar

Speech Simplified
20-22 Wenlock Road
London, UK
N1 7GU

www.speechsimplified.co.uk
www.mohsenalattar.org

CONTENTS

PREFACE

Public lectures are versatile. They inform and inspire, challenge and provoke, stimulate and entertain. I say this with confidence as I consume public lectures as much as I deliver them. Thanks to thousands of hours of public speaking I've logged, I am often described as a captivating and memorable speaker.

In the past year alone, I delivered lectures to the British Council in Singapore, the Chevening Association in Malaysia, and the Beijing Foreign Studies University. These lectures covered topics ranging from legal disobedience to the Chinese-US trade war, from the evolution of NGO activism to the future of international economic law. In all instances, the response from the respective audiences was heartening, but it was also telling. Alongside appreciation for the content, the method of delivery moved my audiences.

Years of feedback have convinced me that successful public speakers are more skilled than talented, that quality public speaking is more technique than art. That is the first contentious message of my book. Charisma, the gift of the gab, and a knack for comedy are useful abilities to possess. There is no denying this. But these are insufficient to deliver captivating talks consistently. Some days, jokes fall flat. On others, charisma crashes into a room of curmudgeons. So, while these abilities are useful, you are mistaken to assume them either essential or sufficient.

The second message is equally controversial. I wish to persuade you that fear of public speaking is not fear at all. Are people anxious when called upon to speak publically? Yes. Public speaking coaches write books and design courses to help amateur speakers manage their fear. However, I dispute the claim that fear is the barrier. Just as people fear speaking in public, they also frighten when interviewing for a job, when answering questions posed by a police officer, or when attending a workplace dinner party. What is common to these events? We are on the receiving end of someone else's gaze and fear being judged.

Imagine walking onto a pitch to play a game of football. Aside from the occasional kick around, you are not a football player. You agreed to help a friend's office team, which found itself short. Little did you know that the team was playing the last match of the season and, as is tradition, players invited family and friends to the game, resulting in an audience of over two hundred spectators. Will you be anxious, frightened even? Undoubtedly. Why? Is there something especially terrifying about playing a game? Does your career hinge on your performance? Will familiars and strangers alike ostracise you for a misstep? Of course not. You are afraid because you do not know what you are doing and worry that you will embarrass yourself. You probably will since the other players have the benefit of experience and team cohesion.

My point here is simple: any activity we must do in front of a large audience will cause us to tense up if we do not know how to do it well. The same is true of public speaking. I may get nervous when standing in a courtroom or lecture theatre, but I know what to do. Even if I lack confidence in the subject or argument, I know how to deliver my speech, what to say, what not to say, and, vitally, how to engage the audience constructively. Even if I cannot convince them, I will not embarrass myself, as I understand the game and can play it to a lofty standard. However, there are activities I am terrible at or have never done before, like a piano recital in a grand hall. Can I play a tune on a piano? Sort of. Would I be comfortable playing a tune in front of a small audience? Not if my life depended on it. I am not a pianist nor a musician. I would crumble if asked to perform music publically.

Your supposed fear of public speaking is not fear at all. It is anxiety borne of unfamiliarity with the task at hand combined with an obligation to carry out the task in front of many watchful and judgmental eyes. Reading this book will familiarise you with techniques that public speakers rely upon. These techniques build confidence as you learn to communicate effectively and efficiently with an audience. Nothing more. By learning these techniques, you will come to appreciate that public speaking is little more than an oral performance delivered to a (mostly) sympathetic crowd. It is not a walk in the park, but it is not brain surgery either. Forget all the talk about fear and focus on learning the techniques and practicing the skills needed to carry out the task well.

Throughout this book, I will show you how to mesmerise your audiences over and over. As flattered as I am to receive the praise that I do, my public speaking skills are much more the result of precise techniques than of innate ability. Effort is essential, to be sure. First as a barrister and second as a professor, I have clocked thousands of hours of public speaking where I honed—and continue to hone—these techniques. However, the adoption of a few simple techniques will ensure that you, too, can captivate and mesmerise your audiences.

1

FEAR IS OPTIONAL

Public speaking fills people with dread. And with good reason. We spend a lot of time communicating with others in conversation (dialogue) and very little time speaking to others without interaction (monologue). In a monologue, we are under the spotlight, perhaps under the microscope. Audiences judge our appearance and clothes, the content and intonation, and our choice of vocabulary. Depending on the context, the audience might be sympathetic to our plight. They can also be unforgiving. We know this because we are in the audience more frequently than the spotlight and are fully aware of the judgmental gaze we cast upon the speaker. It gives us pause for thought, but mostly it gives us pause for trepidation, hence the dread. Even experts are anxious when standing on stage wondering whether the words will roll out smoothly or clunk out in the wrong order. Is there any way of making the exercise less painful? Thankfully, the answer is a resounding yes!

In this book, I provide many techniques to help you improve your rhetorical skills. Let's face it: standing on stage makes for a harrowing experience, but it can be more than just that. Public speaking can also enrich and inspire. Practice helps. But more important than this is the right practice, the kind that will strengthen your confidence and allow you to manage the butterflies while on stage. In due course, you will even learn to use them to your advantage.

You will not automatically become an expert public speaker after reading this. That is impossible! You will, however, gain familiarity with key strategies that, if deployed, ensure that your message reaches the audience as you intend it. Audiences will focus on what they please. If someone spends the length of your talk vetting your clothes or hair, chances are they will not hear much of what you say. However, tools exist to help you capture their attention and refocus their minds on your voice, your words, and ultimately, your message.

This book applies to anyone who engages in public speaking in a professional capacity. Here I have in mind barristers, directors, managers, coaches, business professionals, professors, and salespeople. You may have as little as one hour of experience or ten years' worth to benefit from these strategies. Having scoured the shelves of multiple bookstores for comparable texts, I say this confidently. There are plenty of excellent books on public speaking that you can choose instead of this one. What makes my text unique is the simplicity and retainability of the techniques. I take pride in deploying information in a manner that is accessible and gripping. This ability, too, is central to your progression from raw to skilled speaker.

Is my confidence warranted? The answer lies in both my background and experience. As much as I hate to date myself, I graduated from law school twenty years prior to writing this book. Following my degree, I worked as a barrister, with some success, before embarking on an academic career, with even more success. In total, I have accrued thousands of hours of public speaking experience and, if you believe Malcolm Gladwell's 10,000-Hour Rule from his book Outliers: The Story of Success, I am nearing the world class threshold. Students and colleagues have awarded me more honours than I care to share and I am regularly invited to speak to audiences about a plethora of topics including, you guessed it, public speaking. Perhaps most important of all, it is a craft that I adore. This, despite a shaky start at school.

A quasi-traumatic experience in high school nudged my fascination with public speaking. As part of the assessment for a humanities class, the teacher required me to deliver a 3-minute presentation, in French, on a topic of my choosing. For some odd reason, I opted to speak about aircraft landing signals (!). I wish I could tell you it was a resounding success, that I enthralled my peers with my gestures and utterances, that I mesmerised the teacher, scoring the highest mark in my class. Had any of this happened, my story would differ. It was a disaster. I think the speed of my delivery nearly broke the sound barrier. The only thing my classmates found mesmerising was that I did not drown in my sweat. To add insult to injury, my teacher nearly failed me for missing the 3-minute target (I only managed 2:52).

Contrary to what many believe, I am neither a natural speaker nor a natural communicator. The dread I experienced as a 12-year-old delivering a presentation on landing signals to 25 classmates is loosely the same feeling that descends upon me, albeit briefly now, when lecturing 600 university students. My fascination with the craft propels me to welcome opportunities from across the world and across age groups. Examples are many, but those that stand out include a lecture to school-age children in Los Angeles about Little Red Riding Hood's lawsuit against the Big Bad Wolf and to Singaporean bankers about when they should disobey the law (and, no, the answer is not never). Despite the difficulty of lecturing to diverse audiences on wide-ranging topics, I embrace the challenge. I haven't changed fundamentally. In some ways I'm still that startled 12-year-old. But I have turned a weakness to my advantage and am now skilled in a series of well-tested strategies that will help even awkward speakers become engaging.

Happily, you need not take my word for it. I invite you to visit my podcast, Speech Simplified, or my YouTube channel before deciding whether this book is worth reading. You will find samples of my lecturing collated from a decade's worth of public speaking. I continue adding to them every year. You will notice a variety of distinct styles: some involve the use of notes and others do not, some are light-hearted and others are polemical but, as the feedback suggests, all are captivating and memorable, the two attributes a public speaker should pursue.

What do I hope you take away from this book? While my aim is to teach you strategies to enhance your abilities at public speaking, we can distil the key lesson into a single idea. A journalist once asked Nelson Mandela whether he ever felt fear. He thought this a silly question: 'I am human', he said. Anxiety, fear and trepidation are natural responses to high-pressure situations. An absence of these feelings when pontificating to hundreds is more indicative of a speaker's awkwardness than their presence. It shows a lack of interest in people's response to the speech; a lack of awareness of their feelings and thoughts. As Mandela observed, we need not aspire to the negation of human emotion. Quite the opposite. Strength comes from embracing emotions and developing both mechanism and mindset to mediate them. That is what I hope you will take away from this text: to accept that, even if public speaking continues to provoke anxiety in you, the use of the strategies I describe will help you thrive when standing before others.

*

Before I proceed, let me share a few words with you about what this book will not provide. I will then describe the structure of the book and a proposed reading schedule to help you tackle the material in the most effective way.

When researching this book, I read quite a few others about public speaking. Each was illuminating, and I gained much from the homework. What I found, however, is that these books rely heavily on inspirational anecdotes. They build chapters around individual speakers, their background, and the challenges they overcame, all while celebrating some aspect of their rhetorical ability: passion, discipline, or self-confidence, usually all three. While modelling is a valid strategy, these examples mostly act as filler, building the book around feel-good stories that aim to inspire. This style of writing reminds me of films like Coach Carter or Remember the Titans where an awe-inspiring figure unites a band of misfits, triggering in them feelings of camaraderie, commitment and courage. With all due respect to Carter and the authors, my approach differs.

To be clear, I do not discourage emulating others. I often observe powerful speakers to glean new strategies that I can adopt or adapt. Confucius was on point when he asserted that mimicry is the highest form of flattery. But what are we meant to copy? For example, I recall one author detailing the story of a woman whose legs were amputated at a young age. Despite the tribulation, she became a successful track and field athlete and orthopaedic surgeon. She enthralled the crowd with the might of her story and the passion of her words. I doubt neither the sincerity of the speaker nor of the author but, to be blunt, passion is personal and telling someone to find their passion to become a great public speaker is limiting. Most speakers must speak on topics they do not feel endless passion towards. If her passion produced a memorable speech, I can only sit back in awe and enjoy the show. This book is not about finding your passion—though I hope you do—but about developing the capacity to deliver memorable performances about topics you feel no passion for. Many authors infer that passion is essential. Yet, what type of passion was I meant to feel when speaking to my classmates about air traffic signals? Barristers, professors, and directors routinely speak to audiences about subjects they are not passionate about, yet they do so while captivating. I am more interested in their ability to perform consistently than in the achievements, however memorable, of a few star speakers.

In practical terms, this means that I will keep anecdotes to a minimum. I draw on them, but my focus is not on the speaker's identity or their performance. Instead, I am interested in the techniques and strategies they deploy and their effectiveness in captivating the audience. It is these aspects that I will deconstruct in depth, to provide concrete tools to help you build a strategy to perform well at every opportunity.

Where I rely on anecdotes, I share my own. I do not tell these in the form of war stories or celebrations of my abilities, but as evidence-based techniques that you can learn and practice. I will also speak to the subtext (purpose) and the context (surroundings). Since they are my performances, I am best positioned to convey what I was trying to achieve and how the audiences received my efforts.

I realise this second point is controversial. According to many public speaking coaches, a speaker can never objectively test the audience's response to their performance. A neutral observer is better positioned to provide feedback. I am not convinced. Over the years, while I delivered performances to thousands, I was only formally observed a dozen times. Peer observation is invaluable, but the opportunities are scarce. A speaker who wishes to master their craft must be capable of measuring the success of their methods themselves. In fact, this is one technique that I value above all others: the ability to read the room and adapt. It is an advanced skill. Amateur speakers should avoid paying too much attention to casual yawns or rolling of the eyes. Skeptical smirks can disrupt flow just as affirming nods can provide a false sense of success. The approach I value and detail entails adopting a bird's-eye view: read the room and deploy strategies to shift the mood. In this way, the audience becomes a resource that can assist your performance. You will find greater detail in Chapter 8.

*

I conclude with the key points you will take from this book. First, successful speakers, those who enthrall and provoke us in equal measure, possess two key attributes: they are both captivating and memorable. It is essential to distinguish these characteristics, even if they bleed into one another. Captivating speakers are irresistible, capable of both charming and influencing others. So, how can we be captivating? I admit this is difficult; if it were easy, you would not need this book. However, being captivating is not magic. It requires the sincere deployment of techniques that provoke a predicted reaction in others. An understanding of human psychology is helpful as it enables us to favour supportive practices while minimising obstructive ones. As I explain in later chapters, your choice of language, mannerisms, and pace impinge on your audience's response. Along with other elements, you must account for each of these in your strategy if you are to become captivating. Importantly, I also explain how to cluster these elements so you do not feel overwhelmed.

Much of what I write about being captivating applies to being memorable. Brilliant speakers are memorable not because they say something original or charmed. Rather, they possess the ability to say it in a way that compels you to remember them (and perhaps a little of the message). Consider this little-known fact: spoken information is near impossible to retain, with the average person forgetting 90% of what they hear within the first hour of hearing it. That is a damning indictment of our modern system of education that entreats teachers to monologue to sizeable groups of students. Combined with another fact that I will share shortly, this also hints at the shift in political campaigning we witness today.

We need only stretch back six or seven generations to appreciate the colossal transformation in the dissemination and consumption of information. Take the format for the American presidential debates in the mid-1800s. I'm not exaggerating when I say that these debates were exercises in patience, resolve, and willpower. Candidates had three hours to make their case, followed by a one-hour rebuttal. While this may seem like overkill, during historic days of American democracy, a desire to ensure that the voting demographic had sufficient opportunity to probe the prospective president prevailed.

Today's format differs. If debates take place, we observe a radical erosion of the time allocated to participants. We are now used to seeing two to three-minute outbursts, with each participant doing their best to disrupt, even derail their opponent. Although you'd think a shorter timeframe would make it easier to keep information, even for the astute listener, it is near impossible to discern a policy or a position due to the evasiveness of their answers. Part of this change in approach has to do with shrinking attention spans, a phenomenon consistently observed with each new generation.

There is another reason pithy proclamations are being used to court the electorate. Politicians exploit our inability to retain information. They now favour sound bites over substance, indignation over critique, and conviction over contemplation. The shift is critical. While we celebrated previous messages for their heft, we cherish today's messages for their brevity. Parliaments, once rejoiced as forums for in depth and serious discussion, have morphed into circuses fit for a meme. Communications specialists train politicians to 'stay on message', speaking from a narrow range of talking points, each more inane than the next. Notice how often Donald Trump christens his opponents with a cartoon nickname. These stick more than policies. While this development is ominous for democratic governance, it teaches us two lessons about public speaking.

First, according to Malcolm Gladwell again (Talking to Strangers), we are more likely to believe a message we hear for the first time. Speakers can thus make controversial statements with confidence, for audiences will give them the benefit of the doubt. Not that speakers should abuse the trust of the audience; rather, I am pointing to the mind-set of your audience and how you can use this to your advantage.

Your audience is also critical to the second point. Politicians, like speakers everywhere, must nurture a relationship with the audience. Again, it is not a speaker's words that make them memorable, but the feeling they elicit in the listener. This is easier said than done, and many of the speakers I coach struggle with this one. Yet your audience will find it difficult to remember you if you do not provoke an emotional reaction in them. We easily forget messages; emotions last a lifetime. A simple way to verify this claim is to reflect on the transcendental moments of your life: graduation, the birth or death of a loved one, succeeding or failing at an interview, etc. It is near impossible to recollect the words we spoke or heard in that moment. Feelings, however, are as plain as day. Other than 'I have a dream', what do people remember about Martin Luther King's seminal speech? They remember feeling emboldened and, ironically, patriotic. What do people remember about Malcolm X other than his belief in 'any means necessary'? Again, they remember feeling empowered and inspired or, for his opponents, angry and fearful. The same is true for Barack Obama: we will forever associate him with 'hope and change'. Why? Because he made people feel hopeful that change was around the corner. Each of these speakers is captivating. One phrase can make them memorable. Decades later, they still provoke a reaction. This illustrates why I direct many of my strategies toward these goals.

How will the book unfold? Each chapter details a specific skill allowing for both sporadic and periodic reading. You need not commit days to the text but can instead dip in and out according to your own commitments. In addition, you may read the chapters as clusters if you wish to hone an area of your craft. I wrote the book to flow from beginning to end, but the suggested reading schedule elaborated in Chapter 3 will help you take charge of your learning.

A penultimate point that I cannot overemphasise, is that learning the strategies outlined in this text is best achieved through practice. You can and should practise these skills individually. However, for some, you will make greater gains if you rehearse them in front of others. If you are a student, read this book as part of a group. Settle on a schedule, complete the reading, and then practise the skill together. Do you recall the fact about information retention I shared earlier? We only retain 10% of what we hear. There are two other relevant figures: we recall 20% of what we read and somewhere between 40-60% of what we practice. I recognise that the percentages are abstract, but all of us know it to be true, even self-evident. For example, imagine your favourite sports team preparing for an upcoming championship match by either a) gathering around a television to watch clips of the opposing team, b) studying the profile of each player prepared by the team's technical assistants, or

c) hitting the field and the gym to practice drills and increase their fitness levels. Under ideal circumstances, your team will do all the above and more. However, if a coach had to choose just one, I can't imagine a single coach not selecting the third. Reading the book is edifying on its own, yes, but for those who wish to grow, there is no getting around the importance of practicing the strategies to ensure that you absorb and memorise them. In time, make them your own.

*

For my ultimate point, I would like to end where I began: dread. Dread is an unpleasant feeling. I witness dread often. Both my students and daughter (they are roughly the same age) experience and express it the moment I ask them a question. They fear getting the answer wrong. I can see dread in their eyes and can hear it in their voice. The saddest thing is not the lost learning opportunity, though this too is a shame, but the negative impression they develop toward vocalising ideas. It does not improve. With each additional question posed, the dread intensifies until they eventually avert my gaze or, in the worst instances, avoid me altogether by skipping class or family dinners.

Telling someone not to feel anxiety or dread is not only unhelpful but also condescending. Nobody aspires to these feelings. They wish they would go away as quickly as possible. Feelings are not, however, subject to our whims. They stick to us, even enthrall us. Or do they? Recall Mandela on fear: we need not negate our emotions but to develop the mechanism and mindset to manage them. I enjoy public speaking immensely but I no longer feel dread (though still anxiety) as I have developed a set of strategies that give me confidence when I stand before an audience, whoever they are.

My message to you is simple: reading this book will not make you an expert speaker. It will, however, enable you to achieve confidence in your abilities. That will help placate the dread you might normally succumb to. It will also encourage your audiences to focus on your message rather than your behaviour. Successful public speakers should never worry about their hair.

2

WHY DO I NEED THIS BOOK?

Over the years, three friends have entrusted me with the role of best man at their respective weddings. It is a privilege that warms the heart, providing recognition of the high regard a friend has for your relationship and, possibly, your organisational abilities. We expect a best man to plan the hackneyed bachelor party and all three of my friends had demanding and differing expectations. Our topic, however, is the best man's speech.

While the precise configuration of each celebration varies, the best man eventually holds the mic. Expectations are high and, paradoxically, low. Attendees expect entertainment, the groom anticipates celebration, and the bride prays for stories about something other than her husband's debauched past. Standard best man speeches, the kind available for sale online, will cover a few key components. In no particular order: how the groom and best man met; how the bride and groom met; what the respective parents think of their child's spouse; a funny memory; a lovely memory; and a dubious memory. The speech concludes with a proclamation about them being the ideal couple and a perfect match. Hear, hear!

We have heard this speech before. We also have no recollection of what they said. Alcohol may play a part in impairing our memories, but there is more to it than this. The structure is familiar and bland. If you have heard one best man's speech, you have heard them all. Almost. Some stand out, showing the precise attributes that a speaker should pursue and the ones I will address in this chapter.

*

It is tempting to think talented speakers are just that: talented. Yet, by reducing their ability to natural talent, we undermine our own capacity to replicate their practice or even to surpass it. My friends celebrated my interventions at their weddings for the speeches I delivered. Years later and they still smile at the contribution the speech made to their moment, making the event that much more memorable. But how?

For those not blessed with the looks of Salma Hayek, the charisma of Eddie Murphy, the wit of Ocasio-Cortez, the talent of Daniel Day Lewis, or the intellect of Ha-Joon Chang, we are unlikely to be immediately captivating or memorable. Instead, we must approach both qualities not as manifestations of our personality but of our skills. By so doing, we appreciate that we can learn from them despite our perceived (or real) shortcomings. Here I recall the discovery of the renowned sociologist Marshall McLuhan: the medium is the message. Despite the importance of this platitude, many public speakers overemphasise the message and underplay the medium or, as I will explain shortly, they overemphasise content and underplay style and structure. This is a mistake for an array of reasons, but let me begin with a framework that you can develop and deploy straight away.

Whether for marketing, information, or romantic purposes, most messages comprise Three Ss: substance, structure, and style. Being captivating and memorable requires a balanced approach towards all Ss. Yet, far too often speakers approach the task purely through the first lens, finessing the substantive component and ignoring both the framework and the packaging. Substance, however, can only take you part of the way. Two flaws are evident in a substantive-heavy approach.

First, it demands that a speaker identify muscular content every time they speak publicly. This is impossible. It is for this reason that brides fear the best man's speech: they dig deep for content that will captivate and thus frequently resort to the scandalous. The same is true for directors who, believing their ideas to be original, occasionally earth-shattering, deliver it in monotonous and convoluted forms, presuming that the content suffices to raise the dead. It does not.

Second, over-emphasis on content reduces a public performance to a solo act, rendering the audience peripheral. Consideration of style and structure reflects how that content can capture and involve the audience, transforming an act of listening into an experience. At a concert or a sporting event, performers tie the experience to the interactions between performer and audience . While content is important in stimulating the audience, it is no more important than structure and style. To be captivating and memorable is more technique than personality.

*

To ensure that you balance the Three Ss, always begin by assessing the context. To use a simple example, the context for a barrister in a trial differs from a comedian at an awards night. You must customise the same topic when delivering to a different audience, or for a different purpose. Search for any factors that will influence the planning of your talk. For example, what size is the audience? Are they knowledgeable or neophytes? What is the layout of the room? Can you access a fixed or roving mic? Is a lectern available? While these may seem trivial, each one affects the context and thus influences the quality of your delivery. Consider how restless the audience becomes when a speaker goes over time, pitches their talk at an inappropriate level, or speaks so quietly that the audience must strain to hear them. Context affects not only the suitability of the substance but also of the structure and style, hence why it is your first port of call.

Once you understand context, I suggest tackling structure. How you design your performance will inform its accessibility and thus affect your audience's response. Many of you are familiar with the tenets of storytelling. It is a very effective approach and one that I discuss at length in Chapter 10. For now, I wish to emphasise that structure is key to comprehension and an endless variety of models are available. For example, options include the funnel or reverse-funnel approach (beginning wide before narrowing and vice versa), the mirror model (reflecting the audience's views back to them), the data approach (building the talk around statistics, testimonials, or even definitions), the geographical model (using the shape of land-mass or the locations of cities as guide), or the architectural model (similar to the geographical one except involving a structural frame). I explain these in Chapter 10. A plethora of structures are available to any speaker, ending only at the limits of their imagination. When structuring a talk, it is useful to select two to three models that appear intuitively appropriate and, once we settle content, to choose the one most appropriate. Let me provide an example.

Conference organisers invited me to deliver the keynote lecture at a legal pedagogy symposium at the University of Alberta. The chair of the organising committee requested a talk on student engagement. Engagement, to be clear, is a bugbear for most academics. As the story goes, students disengage from lectures, preferring to occupy themselves with devices rather than professors. How to arrest this trend is the subject of much academic research (and angst). In anticipation of the lecture, I reflected on the context: an academic symposium involving legal scholars and intended to both educate and inspire. After much deliberation, I opted for the spaghetti western model, structuring my talk around seven tips to promote student engagement or, as I titled it, The Magnificent Seven: How Spaghetti Westerns Can Help Us Improve Our Teaching.

I opted for this model for several reasons. First, during symposiums, scholars are often as disengaged as the students they complain about, so I needed a structure that would excite them. Humour is often an effective strategy. Second, the average age of academics at Canadian law schools is over 40, so I could presume familiarity with the spaghetti western genre. And, third, for a talk about student engagement to prove persuasive, I had to be engaging myself. The spaghetti western genre provided me with a captivating and memorable entry point because of the unexpected link between the genre and legal education. In short, even before delivering the talk and, in fact, even before I decided on content, I already had the audience's attention (not to mention that a playful title always helps).

*

With context and structure in hand, move on to style. This is also important before selecting content. Like structure, speakers neglect style. Yet it is essential when seeking to deliver a captivating and memorable talk. The possibilities are endless: expository, inquisitorial, oppositional, comedic, or pugilistic. Each of these styles is appropriate and a skilled speaker will often shift between two, possibly even three styles in the course of a single talk. While I explain style in more detail in Chapters 6 and 12, a few initial thoughts are helpful.

First, style will influence the choices you make around adjectives, metaphors, and illustrations. Style will precipitate an array of emotions from your audience: humorous speakers differ from irreverent ones and even more so from the technical type. Each linguistic device can enhance your performance just as it can hinder it. Not only must you identify a style that is suitable, but you must also align the language accordingly. We should never underestimate style, for it transforms the feel of a performance and is one of the easiest tools for captivating and repelling your audience.

Just this past year, an NGO tasked me with delivering an 'inspirational' talk at an awards gala, organised to commemorate the work of a New Zealand-based charity. Other than an uplifting tone, guidance was sparse. Since this organisation works with the local

Muslim community, I had to account for the massacre that occurred in Christchurch six months prior and the grief that still gripped many of the attendees. Rather than avoid the elephant in the room, I embraced it wholeheartedly, opting for a trinity of styles including shame (I feel embarrassed about delivering an uplifting talk while the bodies are still warm), honour (at being invited to speak at such an occasion precisely because of the context), and pride (at the resilience and resourcefulness of the charity and community in the face of towering adversity). Style was vital in shaping the content, and much of the praise I received afterwards reflected the feelings the style elicited in the attendees: they thanked me for voicing their grief and acknowledging their struggle.

*

It is only at the last stage that you build content. Assuming you follow the steps outlined above, and detailed in the forthcoming chapters, building content will be smooth, almost effortless. Some elements are essential, but by tackling structure and style beforehand, it is easier to discern what is imperative and what we can cast aside. Distinguishing the necessary from the gratuitous is itself a vital skill and, yet again, an area where speakers slip up.

It is common to cover too much ground. This is a direct consequence of leading with content. Seen through this prism, everything appears indispensable, making it nigh on impossible to distinguish between prime cuts and stock ingredients. It feels more like jettisoning the main dish than shrinking the portion sizes. However, with context, structure, and style in hand, it is easier to pinpoint superfluous material that does not cohere with your wider agenda. An example will clarify this point.

In my role as Director of Internationalisation at the University of Warwick, I take part in speaking engagements with a mix of governmental agencies, including the British Council. What makes these events challenging is the uncertainty surrounding the audience. Some attend out of an interest in the advertised topic. Others are anglophiles or wish to be entertained. Going in blind inhibits my ability to know how to pitch the performance. This happened last year when delivering a talk to the British Council's Hong Kong office on the value of a British legal education in a post-Brexit climate. In deciding what to include and exclude, the context, structure, and style guided me. The context was simple enough: widespread uncertainty around Brexit (in September 2019) meant that I could say little with confidence. For the structure, I opted to frame the talk around a contemporaneous conversation I had with my daughter about her future. Once I settled on the context and the structure, the style was plain as day: a combination of exploratory and advisory. I included content about university education and British university education in particular. In line with the topic, I added a section on legal education at Warwick.

Notice how the context allowed me to exclude Brexit from the discussion altogether: rarely is speculation of interest to anyone. Next, by settling on the structure, I determined that general reflections on both university and legal education were in order, as were some on the British tertiary sector. I threw Warwick into the mix, first, as it enhanced my credibility and, second, as it provided plentiful anecdotes I could draw upon. Since I opted for an exploratory and advisory tone, I knew I could riff loosely on some of these topics while also nudging the audience toward criteria they might consider in making future decisions. By reflecting on context, structure, and style beforehand, I drastically narrowed the content choices I needed to make.

*

What I hope this chapter makes clear is that mesmerising audiences demands far less charisma and personality than people presume. Use charisma if you have it, but do not fret if you don't. Instead, plan your talk strategically. The Three Ss is a useful frame. By dividing structure, style, and substance into separate but complementary components, your preparation will be more effective. Your talk will enjoy greater cohesion as you consider each element in relation to the others and select material that will achieve what the audience wants: for you to captivate them. Your talk will be memorable not because of your smashing personality, but because your strategy acknowledges the reciprocity between you and the audience. It affords them a central role in your thinking about the topic and delivery of the talk. Audiences invariably engage more deeply with speakers who make them feel that they are part of a conversation rather than recipients of information.

3

HOW SHOULD I USE THIS BOOK?

Before writing this book, I read several others on public speaking that adorn shelves at major bookstores. Each was useful in its own right. Authors often share stories about powerful speakers, dissecting various parts of their performances. From these narratives, the authors extrapolate tips amateur speakers can adopt to improve their craft. Mimicry is the lynchpin of these texts, as they call readers to emulate the best practices of others. I note, however, that they write very little about their preparations or about their failures (which happen to all of us).

Another common approach reverses the order. Authors begin with the psychology behind speakers and audiences, expounding on practices that stimulate and on those that anaesthetise. They then corroborate their claims with illustrations, case studies, or hypotheticals.

A third form is autobiographical. The author recounts stories about their own experiences of speaking in public: the highs and lows, the memories they cherish, the experiments gone awry, and the lessons gained along the way. Such authors rely heavily on humour as they poke fun at their own consistent misfortune while subtly bolstering their credibility as a master orator. Heavy on anecdote and charm, and light on application, the authors leverage the charisma, personality, and experience of the authors to impart wisdom about public speaking.

Each text is valuable yet flawed. The value is self-evident; whoever is sufficiently patient to complete the text will learn a few precious lessons about public speaking. The texts are also entertaining. I laughed aloud throughout. Sometimes the inspirational characters they describe moved me to tears (recall the amputee athlete and surgeon from Chapter 1). The greatest flaw, however, is the repetitiveness. Heavy on storytelling, readers must sift through a lot of chaff before reaching the wheat. Eventually, each narrative bleeds into the other. Story number twelve is not nearly as stirring. The lessons are also redundant and abstract. We are told to be passionate, whimsical, and creative. This is a tall order for those who must speak frequently and consistently about topics that elicit little passion or vim.

For this book, I adopt a unique approach. There are case studies, illustrations, and war stories. The book would bore without them. What is distinct, however, is that each chapter conveys a single lesson, itself a building block in your quest to become more captivating and memorable. Notwithstanding the initial three chapters, which you have hopefully read in succession, you may read the remaining sequentially or piecemeal. Part 2 elaborates on all matters that pertain to practice, including preparing yourself, your speech, and for your audience. In Part 3, I detail several basic skills ranging from the narrative model of delivery to the tempos you might adopt. Part 4 seeks to teach you advanced skills that you can add to your repertoire, including framing and signalling. While I believe anyone can achieve mastery over all of them, I encourage amateur public speakers to conquer the initial techniques before proceeding to the advanced strategies. For skilled public speakers, you may wish to refresh your practice by browsing through the basic strategies before tackling the advanced ones. In the last part, I wrap up the book by cautioning you against pitfalls and tactics for dealing with the challenges ahead.

*

While I think moving from one chapter to the next is the most sensible approach, I include below a series of clusters for those who want to enhance a specific set of skills.

A- Storytelling: popularised by the Ted talk model, storytelling is the go-to frame for public speaking. What is the secret? A handful of elements are key to an enjoyable story: context, characters, plot, delivery, and crescendo. Storytelling is one of the easiest skills to develop for both speakers and audiences are exposed to them from an early age. Read the following chapters and you will improve your storytelling abilities greatly: 5, 8, 9, and 14.

B- Performance: some speakers already possess a firm grasp of the basics. They know what they need: they can craft a story, read the audience, and close with fireworks. Despite these competencies, their delivery falls flat. The individuals frequently lament their lack of charisma or natural talent. Poppycock. They need to finesse their performance. Chapters 4, 5, 10, 11, and 12 will help these speakers with tone, pace, and movement.

C- Organisation: while many elements can make a performance, the absence of structure will always break it. Most unfortunate for a poorly structured talk is that the speaker commits time and effort into building the content. Where do they go wrong? In chapters 6, 7, 9, and 15, I explain how to organise a lecture in a fluid, accessible, and structured manner. You will learn about the art of preparation, the value of mind-maps, the use of frames and signals, and the ideal way to conclude. Attractive design, consistent delivery, and speedy production are key lessons of these chapters.

D- Interacting: what stands out about my public speaking style is the rapport I develop with the audience. A 30-minute talk is sufficient for an audience to feel that they know me. This adds currency to my talks, for rapport is essential in building trust and enhancing persuasiveness. I wrote chapters 4, 6, 10, 11, and 14 to aid you in developing a similar rapport. From a well-timed smile, pause, or gag, to structural flow, fluidity, and cohesion, each of these elements will help you relate to your audience and enhance your credibility.

E- The Entertainment Society: I design my final cluster for those speakers who wish not just to perform well but to floor their audiences. I admit this is no easy feat. It requires mastery over a mixture of skills and, as is clear from the chapter selection, these are advanced skills. I intend this cluster for those who enjoy a challenge and to challenge their audiences. Getting through these chapters requires patience and perseverance. Most of all, it requires practice. In chapters 5, 6, 10, 11, 12, and 16, I detail the skills that will help you reach beyond being captivating and memorable. By the end of this cluster, you will understand the ingredients needed to mesmerise.

PART 1: HOW TO PREPARE

INTRODUCTION

[The following is an abridged and anonymised account of a conversation I had with a senior colleague.]

Me: Colleague X gave a wonderful talk. It had everything: characters, cliff-hangers, and there was even a denouement involving a grandparent. What a speaker!

Colleague Y: Was it the one about Lauterpacht and Cambridge?

Me: It was! How did you know?

Colleague Y: He's been doing the rounds with that one.

Recall Thomas Edison's quip: genius is 1% inspiration and 99% perspiration. In no field is this assertion more accurate than in public speaking. Colleague X can deliver a mesmerising talk about a deceased legal scholar and an academic research centre because he delivered it two dozen times already, providing him plenty of opportunity to iron out the wrinkles. The jokes, the searching stare, and even the childish smirk when imitating a grandparent, were all rehearsed, performed, and perfected. And who would blame them? Pilots practice in simulators; surgeons practice on cadavers; and politicians practice before speech coaches. Improvisation is an essential skill, to be sure, and I discuss this later in the chapter, but far more vital than an ability to think on your feet is a commitment to practice. Practice is part of your preparation and no capable orator would deliver a talk without preparing (while the best ones will make it seem off-the-cuff).

How to prepare? As you will quickly learn, I believe in systems. I believe in systems not because I fetishize order—though my A-type personality means I do—but because systems provide useful frameworks for thought and action. Within this framework, we require a mixture of skills, technique, and even intuition. The framework, however, establishes the parameters we work within, providing us with a pathway to greater efficiency and impact. Four elements are essential to your preparation: audience, space, speaker, and speech. I will deal first with the three elements you enjoy the greatest control over, followed by the one you have a little less influence over (the audience).

4

THE SPEAKER

Public speaking begins and ends with the speaker. We are privileged with the first and final words, and we hold the greatest sway over ourselves. When lecturing on rhetoric or when coaching speakers, I place much emphasis on the individual. A range of strategies and techniques can transform your presentation style, helping you build greater rapport with your audience. You are never in control of what the audience pays attention to, but you can nudge them to respond positively to your message.

To begin, this means accounting for your own abilities while preparing. What are your strengths and weaknesses? Will you share the stage with others, whether chairs, panellists, or antagonists? If so, how will their strengths and weaknesses reflect on you? Gerry Spence, the renowned trial lawyer, is infamous for sending assistants to monitor his opponents in action. While lawyers often cried foul, he was doing what every other lawyer should do: determine their game plan based upon the opposition they face. It would be negligent and counter-productive to engage opponents without assessing their abilities. The same is true for you. Public speakers must know themselves before they can play the game. An excellent habit is to practice in front of a mirror and to record and watch yourself. Unless we observe ourselves in action, we limit our ability to identify our strengths and weaknesses and to remedy our flaws.

How should you look? Observe all aspects of yourself: clothes, mannerisms, hand gestures, ticks, and anything else that stands out. You should put aside both vanity and humility. The point is to evaluate your appearance and personal presentation style to improve where needed. While style and appearance are highly personal, there are some general rules. None of these will make or break your talk, but they affect your credibility and the audience's attention.

In evaluations by students and clients, I am harangued for my beard ('too groomed'), my bald patch ('you are ageing'), my fashion style ('too hipster', 'too formal', and 'too [add your preferred criticism here]') ... need I go on? Obviously, I handpicked the comments that drive the point home. Remember, individuals noticed these elements during the lectures I delivered. I am neither a model nor an actor; I am not someone whose appearance should matter to audiences. But it does, and audiences are brutal when judging speakers.

I am sympathetic to the resentment speakers feel towards this. Nobody enjoys being judged by strangers. But the audience will judge you, and ruthlessly at that! And, for the record, audiences are far harsher towards women and people of colour, who must deal with an array of systemic biases. Save yourself the grief by sticking to five basic guidelines that will neutralise some bad blood.

DRESS THE PART

One of two aesthetic styles is suitable for any speech: business casual or formal (you should draw the line just before the black tie). This rule applies to financiers as it does to football coaches. Both styles convey a mixture of qualities that enhance your credibility. We deem speakers who dress professionally as more respectful and thoughtful. We hold such speakers in higher esteem, verifying that clothes can make the person. Why is this?

Clothes are more than material objects. They are symbols devised to convey characteristics about the wearer, including personality, politics, and social status. We ascribe value to pieces of clothing, as aesthetics can convey a range of messages. For example, bankers value Brooks Brothers clothing more than band members and bebop artists. The same is true for other styles that resonate with or repel certain sub-cultures. A CFO I worked with covered his wrist tattoo with a watch. Appearance—including clothing—operates as a semiotic code. Your identity and your audience's perception of your identity intermingle in your outfit. A speaker can make a statement with their clothing just as they can opt for something more innocuous and leave the audience guessing. Not subscribing to any obvious subculture, I prefer business casual or formal, depending on the event.

I admit I know a few professionals who sport T-shirts, hoodies, and even lycra cycling shorts in public speaking settings (the latter is as bad as it sounds). None of this is appropriate. Contrary to what the cool kids think, you gain no points for credibility by underdressing. Returning to studies on the subject, the immediate effect of underdressing is to lessen your credibility among audiences. They do not take kindly to sloppy dressers, asking themselves: if you cannot bother dressing appropriately, why should we bother listening to you? I do not blame them. You seek their attention and, at a minimum, should treat your appearance with care.

I make one last remark on dress: colour matters. Advertisers have perfected the use of colours to elicit mood and precipitate behaviour. While people interpret colours differently, and that preferences and associations vary across cultural and social groups, young audiences prefer vivid colours, while their older counterparts prefer subdued ones. Tendencies exist, and these can be used to your advantage or your detriment in equal measure. For example, turning up to an Indian funeral to deliver a eulogy while dressed in black would be thoughtless (white is the colour for mourning in India). Rarely will you make a misstep of this magnitude by choosing traditional or muted colours, but neither will you make any friends. Just as you should align your outfit with the occasion, dedicate a few moments to selecting a colour scheme that will strike the right tone.

BRING MATERIALS AND PROPS

Do not underestimate the power of props. I always carry and display a document or device (a laptop is better than a phone) when speaking. Your prop should be both clear and inconspicuous. You don't need to show the audience your materials, but they should have confidence in your preparation. Audiences are sympathetic toward those who try but be careful not to overdo it. Just as presentations of 10 slides or more are overkill, so too is a raft of materials awkward and liable to make you look disorganised and ill-prepared. Chapter 11 on mind-mapping will ensure that you arrive with appropriate support.

Should you prepare a PowerPoint or Prezi? This issue arises constantly, as slides are now compulsory in the minds of most. So ubiquitous is the practice that every time I arrive to deliver a talk, the organisers request my USB presuming I have slides to display. Are these necessary? The curt answer is no. The long answer is that it depends.

Arguments against the pervasiveness of PowerPoint are abundant. I will mention two. First, slides presuppose that information travels in a linear trajectory; in fact, slides demand it. The format you adopt to convey information will alter how your audience receives it. For example, a discussion about the evolution of the Internet delivered via slides will infer that each step was sequential and deliberate. In fact, anyone familiar with the development of the Internet will understand that multiple teams were working separately on aspects of the framework. Each ripened at unique points in time, precipitating a critical mass of capacity that led to the establishment of the Internet and, subsequently, the World Wide Web. It was organic, unpredictable and uncoordinated. Even now, various activities continue to happen both intentionally and inadvertently, such is the nature of scientific development. The linear nature of slides, however, leaves an impression that the evolution was neat, structured even. PowerPoint's ubiquity has foisted a contrived format upon all information.

Second, as I explain in more detail in Section D below, your audience has a burdensome task. Listening to a speaker is hard work. It is too easy for our minds to wander. By providing your audience with a focal point other than yourself, you enable their wandering. Each time a new slide appears, the audience shifts from listening to looking and reading (text-heavy slides are the worst kind). Not only must they engage in a different activity, but they also swing their attention elsewhere. Try an experiment: ask someone to explain something to you and, one minute into their response, turn away and look out a window. Return to the speaker a few seconds later and repeat this act several times. Assess your level of focus at each transition point. You'll require a moment to observe the image and another to refocus on the speaker. Distraction is inevitable as slides prompt the audience to suspend listening.

We can marshal more arguments against slides, but these two suffice. Are slides ever advisable? First, if you are explaining nuclear fusion. Slides are useful for technical speeches that require sophisticated diagrams, graphs, or statistics. In these instances, visual depictions help the audience process complex information. An explanation about nuclear fusion delivered in narrative form will be incomprehensible to all but nuclear physicists. Slides have their place when they illustrate—rather than to deliver or explain—information.

This brings me to the second instance where slides are advisable: when comprising a single word or simple image that complements your point. Here slides play a mnemonic role that renders information more accessible and engaging. Words and images do not distract but focus the mind on the point under examination. Sight is a vital source of information. You can improve your effectiveness as a speaker if you prepare slides that illustrate parts of your speech. Timing is everything, and you must rehearse to ensure that the slides appear on cue.

MAKE EYE CONTACT

Eyes are windows into the soul. Opening up to the audience will make you endearing. We do this by making eye contact consistently and sincerely. I am astonished how many speakers neglect this act.

One outstanding scholar of banking law is so well versed in his field he requires no notes to deliver exhilarating lectures. He mixes sophisticated exposes of the regulations with topical case studies, metaphors, and even personal anecdotes. Despite his proficiency, attendance hovers around 30% with students actively avoiding his lectures. He asked me to observe him in action and pinpoint what he's doing wrong. I needed less than a minute to spot the problem: he makes no eye contact with his audience. In fact, not only does he not make eye contact, he is avoiding eye contact. In the hour lecture, I counted five occasions where he glanced in our general direction. For the rest, he scrutinised the floor, his hands, the ceiling, space, and just about everything except the audience. It was surreal and, despite my best efforts, I too drifted. Every time it distracted me, I stopped listening to the lecture. While he is an extreme example—and, thankfully, has since corrected his behaviour—failure to make eye contact will disconnect you from your audience.

A subsequent gaffe is equally disconcerting. Unbeknownst to most, we favour particular directions with our eyesight and repeat these habits when in public; I look left and up. Rarely will anyone notice this subtle tendency, unless you are delivering a public performance. When speaking to an audience, this habit produces an imbalance in the distribution of attention. Audience members we neglect can quickly become resentful as they perceive us to favour others. We don't and are merely succumbing to habit, unfortunately, truth matters little to a jilted audience. We must spread eye contact to every member of the audience, or at least to every section of the room. Cast your net wide and let your gaze meet as many people as you can. Maintain contact for two to three seconds before hopping to the next. Do not ignore those at the back. Finally, you should be cautious not to overdo it with a single audience member. Though you might perceive them as a safe point, it will upset everyone else.

I stress this point as few behaviours are more influential to the audience's perception of you than eye contact. Your effort to connect with the audience will endear you to them as quickly as your failure to do so will alienate you.

MOVE PURPOSEFULLY

Recall the statistic I shared earlier: 90% of communication is non-verbal. Movement plays a key role in conveying any message, especially in large audiences where the totality of your performance will dictate how they receive you. This makes sense: it is far easier for people to remain engaged in a discussion when it takes place either one-to-one or in small groups. In these situations, the conversation will end promptly if the speaker notices the other drifting or playing on their phone, common occurrences at speaking events. In one-to-one conversations or small group discussions, your gestures may entertain but they will not win or lose you any friends. The opposite is true for movement and mannerisms before large audiences. In these instances, movement can both enhance and undermine your performance.

It is important to distinguish between purposeful and habitual hand gestures. Habitual gestures are self-explanatory. We do not notice them. However, when practicing public speaking, we must try to recognise our patterns. All movement will affect your audience's perception, hence it pays to know which habits are benign and which are noxious. While there are no hard and fast rules, useful benchmarks to reflect on are speed, scope, and frequency. Reduce the speed of your movement as quick successions of gestures are jarring. The same is true for overly elaborate and grand gestures, more suited to method actors than public speakers. Overacting is useful in limited situations, but use this practice sparingly lest you appear the buffoon. For now, reduce the range of your gestures. Finally, keep your gestures to a moderate number. What is moderate? Over one movement every three or four seconds and you are treading close to danger; over one every two seconds and you have crossed the line.

Reducing speed, scope, and frequency is sensible in all circumstances. Let me remind you that the audience's task is more difficult than yours. Public speakers demand that audiences a) sit still, b) quietly, c) for an extended period, and d) while listening deeply. I feel no animosity towards individuals who tire during my lectures, for listening is hard work. Erratic gesturing—whether too fast, big, or frequent—will further exhaust the audience. It forces them to follow not only your words and message but also your movements.

There are two ways of determining whether your habitual hand gestures are overwhelming your audience. First, record and watch yourself. This is the easiest way of identifying any annoying habits you possess. Second, and I prefer this approach, deliver a 20-second segment of a speech two-to-three times consecutively. In the first round, your performance is raw and coated with any lingering anxiety. Your movements will be as brusque as they will be. As you ease into it the second and third times, you will relax and naturally reduce the speed, scope and frequency of your gestures. We tend towards these manners when uncomfortable, using them to compensate for our nerves. Whichever gestures remain by the third round are less intrusive on your performance.

I have much more to say about movement, including positive ways of enhancing your speech through animation and association. I dedicate Chapter 14 to this topic. Impatient thespians may wish to skip ahead but the advice in this section will satisfy most.

PERFORM LIKE AN ACTOR

Actors possess two abilities that I admire: first, to get into character and, second, to change characters with the ease of changing shirts. As Charles, an actor friend, explained to me, this is what they practice. He works his craft tirelessly, running through distinct moods, identities, and reactions. I have seen Charles experiment at cafes when ordering a coffee or speaking with the person next to him. He ponders how he can reflect each of these elements in his facial expressions, intonations, or mannerisms. For example, a character with acute anxiety is unlikely to punch the air in triumph. By playing with characters, by exploring the breadth of their behaviour, Charles becomes more fluent in a range of personas. He can 'get in character' at the drop of a dime.

As is clear, I treat public speaking as a performance. When planning my speech, I thus consider which character is most suitable for the role. Some students cringe at the suggestion of playing a part. Can we not just be ourselves? Return to Charles or any actor for that matter. He layers himself in each performance. It is always him, but him in character. Directors cast him not solely for his ability to play someone else but his ability to play someone else as only he can. Johnny Depp or Salma Hayek inject themselves into their roles whether they are playing a bookseller, a pirate, or even a vampire. It is what they bring to the role as Johnny and Salma that earns them the role of Jack Sparrow (Pirates of the Caribbean) and the Muse (Dogma).

In a public speaking context, you need not be someone else altogether. For all talks, however, it is taking two steps. First, reflect on the preferred tone for your performance: gregarious, reflective, combative, melancholic, or inspirational? Next, associate the tone with a character, whether real or imagined. Both steps will ensure that you stay in character throughout. I have a small Rolodex of alter egos I refer to during my preparation. They have names and personalities; some have habits and partialities. The more real I can make them, the more authentic my delivery will be.

Authenticity is key. While choosing a character seems like the ultimate expression of inauthenticity, we are complex beings. Over the past week, our moods have varied. At no point were we not ourselves. We are no more authentic when happy or sad, confident or insecure. We do not always control our feelings, but on the public speaking stage you are more effective when deploying your emotions strategically to create the desired mood.

*

Throughout this book, I show that quality public speaking results from the consistent application of precise techniques. Combined, these facilitate greater engagement with your audience and stimulate a more powerful memory of you. In short, being captivating and memorable is a skill; not a gift.

We therefore need strategic effort to improve. Align your outfit with your image; choose your materials and props carefully; be sincere when making eye contact with audience members; move with purpose; and perform like Al Pacino. You possess creative control over these elements. I reiterate what I wrote in the introduction: you can never command what the audience pays attention to. However, the use of these techniques will increase the probability that they respond positively to your message.

5

THE ART OF PERFORMING

Alongside knowing yourself, you must 'know your performance'. To reiterate a point made in the preface, public speeches serve many purposes. Counter-intuitively, delivering information is not the central one. Knowing your performance differs from knowing your field of expertise. Many experts are rock stars in their respective areas. While this is useful when preparing a speech, subject expertise does not translate into a captivating and memorable talk. In fact, expertise can sometimes be a liability as it provides a false sense of confidence: the speaker presumes themselves competent because of their knowledge.

Below, I provide several concrete tips to ensure that you deliver a successful performance. Before, however, let me identify three missteps that you should avoid under all circumstances. These three practices provide the illusion of preparation but are ultimately sure-fire ways of sabotaging your performance.

WHAT NOT TO DO

First, do not memorise your speech. I have witnessed people do this before and, while it is an impressive talent, the delivery feels contrived and inflexible. Since you've committed to a script, you do not have scope to adjust your speech. You have handicapped your-self. Your audience will reveal important information to you as the speech unfolds (more on this in Chapter 16), yet it is difficult, if not impossible, to deviate from your script. Memorise the outline, format, order, and even case studies you will rely upon; however, always develop your performance in actual time.

Second, do not read your speech to your audience. While this is common for politicians, academics, and some CEOs, it virtually always falls flat. Academics are especially notorious for reading their work. I have watched dazzling academics present fascinating scholarship in the most dreadful way: reading either their articles or condensed versions of them. The impact is instantaneous and devastating. With an inaudible (sometimes vocal) sigh, attendees nestle into their seats in anticipation of the long haul ahead. Only on rare occasions will the audience survive past the initial minutes, becoming distracted along the way. Reading is a brutal practice that will rapidly earn you the audience's ire.

Third, mistakes happen and problems arise: you may feel inar-ticulate, an audience member might disrupt you, overhead projec-tors break down. Preparing for the unforeseen is difficult, so treat this more than a matter of risk management. All the above happened to me and on multiple occasions. How is this a misstep? Surely, we are not responsible for circumstances beyond our control. True, but capable public speakers don't presume that things will go well. Quite the contrary, they prepare contingency plans and techniques for overcoming obstacles. During an advocacy workshop, a youth-ful attendee stopped shortly after beginning, apologised, berated herself, and asked to start over. This is a misstep. Her reaction to the mistake was more damaging than the mistake itself (she merely fumbled over her words). Instead, if she ignored the slip or made a joke of it, she could have carried on with confidence. Your office, study or bathroom is a safe space to trial strategies for dealing with hiccoughs. Rehearse how you will paper over slip-ups. If you do not, you are liable to resort to the apology. Apologies lead to pity, and pity makes you look and feel weak.

To recap, do not memorise your speech, do not read your speech, and do not presume that your speech will go off without a hitch. Avoiding these missteps will get you that much closer to delivering it effectively.

WHAT TO DO

Now that we have reflected on what not to do, let us shift towards positive ways of getting to know your speech. Committed to systems as I am, I divide speech preparation into five elements: a) synthesis, b) structure, c) content, d) tone, and e) avatar. While I explain each do not treat them as mutually exclusive. Each element will affect the other.

SYNTHESIS

I begin by synthesising my speech into a single phrase; the simpler the better. The synthesis forms the nucleus of my talk. I can frame it as a question I will answer, a position I will argue, or an idea I will explore. Treat the synthesis as the headline: it frames your speech and provides a thread you can weave through it. By threading a single idea from beginning to end you a) simplify the audience's engagement with your speech and b) ensure that your speech is cohesive. Your synthesis should operate on two levels: what is the core message of your speech and what action are you trying to provoke? Both are essential to your effectiveness.

Your core message is what you want attendees to walk away with:

1. Privatising healthcare undermines access
2. Your wireless speakers produce better bass
3. Public speaking is a mixture of art and technique

The core message is the metaphorical and literal seed of your speech. You must water it with the other four elements—structure, content, tone and avatar—to blossom. Ultimately, the seed is the most vital element as the others can only nurture what you plant; whether you're growing a banana or a bonsai depends on the seed. In fact, you must tailor the other elements accordingly. Both bonsais and banana plants need water, but to varying degrees.

Surrounding the seed is the 'soil' or the action you wish to provoke. Return to the three seeds above: which action can we associate with each message?

1. If you wish to maintain your access and the access of others to healthcare, sign this petition opposing further privatisation.
2. On Black Friday, pick up a pair of our wireless speakers; they've got better bass than other brands.
3. Since public speaking is both art and technique, you will improve through study and practice.

Notice that I can link the message to an array of actions. To take a self-serving example, public speaking is a mixture of art and technique. I can teach you both so sign up to one of my workshops. Although the action can vary, it is essential to articulate some action lest you leave the audience wondering what you want from them. For example, in legal practice failure to introduce the action can undermine your client's interests. In a courtroom, the action is always more important than the message: find the defendant not guilty, disregard this witness, or compensate the victim. The configuration of message and action varies, though certain messages align better with specific actions. Think about both before finalising your synthesis.

Reveal your message at the earliest moment and restate it at the end. This will get it across. For the action, however, contemplate being circumspect. Days of hard selling are over. Audiences are much more discerning, cynical even. Familiarity with fake news, scams, and media manipulation have left them sceptical toward direct calls to action. To sidestep their suspicion, massage the action into your speech, almost as inception, to borrow from the Christopher Nolan film. Even if you nudge a little, attendees that reach the action you were leading them towards are more likely to commit than those you lasso and drag behind you. Angle, hint, and infer.

You should appreciate that the potential number of messages and actions is countless. If you identify what you want to achieve, you are much better placed to translate this into a message and action that will connect with your audience.

STRUCTURE

With synthesis in hand, your next step is to establish a skeletal structure. Think of this through the lens of construction: high rises differ from single-family homes; mansions differ from townhouses. Each houses people but the variation in structure is tied to the unique circumstances and preferences of the dwellers. The same is true for speeches. They require structures befitting the situation including message, audience and mood (mine). I draw on common structural 'shapes' when developing a suitable outline: the aim is to identify a shape that will help you visualise the contours of your speech and thus provide you with a useful tool for developing familiarity.

From experience, the three most common shapes are the funnel, reverse funnel, and hourglass. Though the shapes are self-explanatory, in due course you will come to appreciate that unique shapes serve distinct types of speeches. Let me explain each.

The funnel is an effective structure when delivering rigorous or technical talks to an amateur or intermediate audience. By opening with a wide picture, you capture their attention. Next, gradually funnel them towards the intricacies of the subject. For example, I recently listened to a talk about the cannabis marketisation model practiced in Canada. While the speaker was obviously an expert in the field, also evident was the ignorance of the audience. It was a town hall meeting involving community members curious about the implications of the law change for their neighbourhoods. Experts were present also but the speaker pitched the talk to neophytes. He began by introducing the topic—narcotics and cannabis regulation—and three unique approaches operating in states around the world: prohibition, legalisation, and marketisation. After briefly defining each and highlighting their positive and negative impacts, he narrowed the contours of his talk, declaring that he would only speak to the marketisation model as they practice it in Canada. By the end of his 5-minute introduction, we understood a little about narcotics, about distinct regulatory approaches, and about their implications. We knew what the speech was about and could focus on the topic at hand—cannabis markets—with the benefit of context.

The reverse funnel is useful when speaking to expert audiences. Experts are familiar with the context and prefer direct engagement with the details. In these instances, it is useful to begin with the issue as experts understand it. Returning to the marketisation of cannabis example, a speech using this structure may begin as follows: 'what policymakers wonder is whether increased accessibility to cannabis because of marketisation increases consumption? Prohibitionists believe this to be the case, but how convincing is their evidence? Their data suffers from two flaws.' Notice that context remains relevant, but I only use it in passing to advance the technical discussion. Experts want to hear about a precise issue and not the more searching talk that a public audience expects. Expanding towards the end, however, is essential in ensuring that they grasp the significance of your intervention and walk away with a memorable point they can share with others.

I reserve the hourglass for occasions when I want to captivate the audience. Opening and closing wide ensures that the speech is accessible and engaging to a diverse demographic. Here you presume neither knowledge nor interest in the nuances of a debate. The hourglass is best suited for introductory lectures or what some mock as 'edutainment': Ted talks, documentaries, and even product launches (see Steve Jobs). In all instances, your aim is to stimulate your audience with grand narratives. So I reserve hourglasses for big occasions, large audiences, and rousing renditions. It is the antithesis of what we should deliver at a job interview (as my previous slip-up confirms).

Just as there are many shapes, there are many structures you can rely upon: the Mayan temple (building blocks), the sand dial (granular), the solar system (rotational), and many more. Your imagination is key. Think of the structure that best characterises your talk and build it accordingly. However, be wary of rash judgement. For example, many presume that a sales pitch always compels going big. In fact, you must massage the message to suit the relevant elements. A sales pitch can just as easily be a reverse funnel (when selling engineering equipment to an aviation company) or a solar system (when pitching to several interdependent stakeholders). Be creative and the right structure will find you.

CONTENT

Counter-intuitively to many, I build content after settling on the structure. You may identify the structure after settling on the content, so long as you adjust your content afterwards to suit the structure that you settle upon. What do I mean by this? Return to my construction metaphor: if the structure is the building plan, the content represents all the materials you will rely upon. Irrespective of which materials you may already possess, you will only use the materials necessary when building. Store everything else for another day. Who would want to squander precious materials if they can build the structure without them? The answer: most public speakers do!

The greatest shortcoming of the vast majority of speeches is a cavalier approach towards content: speakers talk too much. Nine out of ten speakers will overload the audience with far more content than they can process, undermining their persuasiveness. Yet, with public speaking, the adage 'less is more' rules the roost. Consider the following statistic: most people will only remember 10%

of what they hear within 60 minutes of hearing it. Translated, this means that most of your audience will forget 90% of the content shortly after you say it. Content rarely wins the race.

Do not misunderstand me: content is important. It is essential that you do your homework and ensure that your content is accurate, current, and relevant. Most audiences have little sympathy for speakers who rely on inaccurate information and are positively scathing towards those who try to deceive them (partisan political spaces excluded). You can recover from an exaggerated statistic, but an incorrect one will undermine your credibility. During a talk about elitism in the Supreme Court of the USA, I boldly declared that two law schools—Harvard and Yale—provided virtually all the justices to the court over the past two generations. I based this claim on a talk I heard a few weeks prior and a statistic I thought I remembered accurately. I failed to do my due diligence and quoted hyperbole. In fact, Harvard and Yale have provided most justices, but so too has Columbia. After these three, the representation of other law schools plummets. That my claim about elitism in law schools holds true does not matter one iota: following a challenge by an attendee, the audience will remember that I was wrong. If I misrepresented this, they will wonder what else I got wrong and my stock value crashes accordingly.

Bar this type of error, content will rarely sink you. Audience disengagement is far worse, a common occurrence when speakers drone on endlessly. It is always better to leave your audience enthralled and wishing that you had more time than clamouring for the Q&A to begin or, worse, for the curtain call.

To ensure that you achieve balance, build content around the structure. Practice under genuine conditions, delivering the speech in the same way you intend on performing it before your audience. Once you hit your time target, cull 20% of your content. By culling, you will eliminate superfluous material and ensure you deliver your talk to time (nerves cause almost everyone to ramble). Moreover, by forcing yourself to be more discerning about content, you're allowing space to add metaphors, case studies, illustrations, and other devices that will make your talk more lively and memorable.

TONE

In both lawyering and lecturing, practitioners are remarkable in their ability to get the tone wrong. For example, the audience is never your opponent, yet colleagues routinely adopt a combative mindset. Fear of being the pushover is so prominent that their tone becomes short, even pugilistic: you will listen to me, damn it! I assure you they will not, and no amount of coercion will make them. The opposite is also true. Pandering to your audience is an ineffective strategy. In most instances, you will face a diverse audience so pandering to one demographic is liable to alienate you from another.

Tone is more about you and your speech than it is about the audience. Do not misunderstand me: always account for your audience. But remember that audiences are variable and thus a poor benchmark when identifying a suitable tone. Instead, decide the tone according to your message, the action you wish to engender and your personality as a speaker.

Personality is easiest. Recall from the preface: some have the gift of the gab and others do not: some are extroverts and others introverts; some crumble in front of an audience and others come alive. While the techniques in this book will help you improve at public speaking, nothing I say will change your personality. There is no need to. Save for those who suffer from phobias that would prevent them from speaking at a public event, almost all personality types have qualities that can enhance a performance. The examples are plenty. Strong and serious individuals bring gravitas; playful types add levity; and empathetic individuals pull at our heartstrings. Since there isn't a natural tone to a speech, the individuals who possess these personalities can exploit their strengths under the right circumstances. If you reflect on your personality honestly, you will know which qualities you can draw upon.

Next is the action you wish to trigger. Let me explain this point with an example. A friend works as an estate agent and, like some of his peers, attended a Tony Robbins event to boost his career. While my friend expected to learn something, he is no fool and saw this as a one time splurge aimed at developing new skills and building his network. By the end of the weekend, however, he was racing to the front of the queue to register for a follow-up course. Why? When the emotions wore off, and he came to his senses, my friend confessed that the speeches were all delivered with the same tone: buoyant exuberance! All attendees, including him, were in high spirits from the moment they walked in until the moment they walked out, their wallets much lighter for the experience. He recalled little about the actual talk and far more about the feelings he experienced: devotion, exhilaration, and self-confidence.

Clear from this anecdote and from Robbins' infomercials is his aim: his performance targets persuading you to buy products from within the Robbins ecosystem. He couches the commodities in the language of aspiration, self-improvement, and well-being. However, it is nothing more than a sales pitch and the action he tries to elicit is a slide of the credit card. Buoyant exuberance can warm even the curmudgeon's heart, a sure-fire way to loosen the purse strings. Identify and prepare to strike the tone most suitable in engendering the action you desire and you are that much closer to captivating (or hoodwinking!) your audience.

The last element in our triumvirate is the tone of the message. In contrast to your personality or the action you wish to elicit, use the synthesis to inform the tone of the message. For example, if your message is that our executive pay packages abuse shareholder goodwill, a tone of buoyant exuberance would be out of place. The synthesis and the content compel a more meditative tone, perhaps an apologetic one. Assuming you are one of the executives, the audience will expect contrition. If you are delivering the keynote at the AGM, you must follow your mea culpa with a coherent and measured reform programme.

Messages align with a variety of tones and conflict with plenty more. Just as you must discern when choosing the tone of your message, you must also strategise when aligning tone with personality and action. These elements will combine to help you connect with your audience.

AVATAR

As a last consideration when preparing your speech, I include an odd element: avatars. The word avatar sticks out like a leaning tower. What do I mean by avatar and why is it relevant?

My meaning merges the two most common definitions, Hinduism excluded. Online gamers know avatars as characters created to represent a user. In the World Wide Web, photos feel passé so many users adopt avatars as visual representations of their personas. What this first definition captures is the value of an avatar in representing the self as you wish others to see you: an avatar can closely mimic your image or it can depart widely.. The second definition is equally relevant as it explains the association between an avatar and an idea. An avatar embodies what we want others to acknowledge about us. In this way, an avatar symbolises our aspirations, maybe even our ideal self (more on this in Chapter 19).

Returning to my earlier explanation of mnemonics, we are hardwired to learn by association. Thus, you will feel better prepared for your speeches if you develop the habit of representing them with an avatar. The avatar is far more than a reflection of your personality but an embodiment of your persona as it relates to the speech. The avatar you select can help you connect to your speech personally. An example will help allay the uncertainty this topic often provokes.

I was a barrister and am now an academic whose research and teaching focuses heavily on international economic law. My politics, as some of you may have already noticed, would align better with certain political parties, ethical standpoints and personalities than with others. Yet, in both professions (and in my coaching), I connect with a range of people. How do I manage? When preparing my talks, I always envision the persona I wish to convey and visualise it as an avatar that I either illustrate or describe in my notes.

In the talk on legal pedagogy and the spaghetti western genre, my avatar was of an Egyptian cowboy, part Salah al-Din (Saladin) and part Django. It was a difficult avatar to concoct but, once I had it, my persona was clear: disciplined and relentless. My avatar for the speech on the evolution of NGO activism was far different. For this latter talk, I imagined myself as the comic book character Two-Face: half-protestor holding a fist up and half-politician sporting a double-breasted suit. The split personified the struggle I feel exists within activism: smash and subvert on one hand and reform and reorganise on the other.

Two-Face is a very different persona from the one I display when lecturing on the World Trade Organisation. Depending on whether I deliver an undergraduate or postgraduate course, and whether it is doctrinal or critical, my avatars vary accordingly. Sometimes my avatar wears a blue suit and red tie (the WTO negotiator), other times he is wearing an Agbada (the Third World official), and other times he is in indigenous clothing (the opponent), metaphorically. To be clear, these avatars are not based on personal experience. Some characteristics are representative—bearded and dark-skinned—but I am neither a subsistence farmer nor a trade negotiator, I am not a politician nor did I live in the Wild West. Each avatar helps me get into character, allowing me to know my speech better and pitch it in the appropriate tone.

*

So, how should you prepare for future performances? First, the dos and don'ts are equally important. Don't memorise your speech; don't read your speech; and don't presume your talk will go well. The first two missteps will bore your audience to tears. They are the antithesis of being captivating and memorable. They may remember you, but for all the wrong reasons. The final misstep will make you look like an amateur. Developing your ability to adapt to changing and challenging circumstances will ensure that you handle obstacles with ease, bolstering your credibility along the way.

Second, what should you do to prepare? I detail my five key tips above.

- Always synthesise your speech into a single phrase
- Develop a skeletal structure to support your speech
- Build content liberally but cull ruthlessly
- Account for the tone of the message and the action you wish to engender
- Associate your speech with a persona you embody and convey to your audience.

Combined, these preparatory steps will ensure that you stand out in relation to everyone else vying for your audience's attention. While this may seem like a fair bit of work, I remind you of my opening quote: genius is 1% inspiration and 99% perspiration. Being captivating and memorable is not easy. While I hate to dispel the romanticism, those few individuals who captivate us and who we remember have prepared themselves to be so. A speech delivered a dozen times with constant improvement of the elements identified above will be far better than a speech delivered just once and off-the-cuff. Know your speech and your audience will want to know you.

6

THE SPACE

Knowing your space is vital when preparing a performance. Will it be in a lively town hall or a sombre courtroom? Do you have access to technology or old school blackboards? What is the projected size of your audience and what proportion of the seats will remain empty? While answers to these questions are not always forthcoming, they will help you prepare. For example, the quality of my performances diminishes if I must use a handheld or fixed microphone. As someone who gesticulates and meanders, I am handicapped by these types of mics. When faced with these options, I usually forego the mic and project my voice instead. Knowing that I must bellow the performance requires a different mind-set than if I were speaking to a small gathering, hence the importance of obtaining information early on.

When invited to deliver a talk, I pose plenty of questions about the space. Key questions include the ones mentioned, but there are others: how much natural light should I expect? What colour are the walls? Is noise from the projector's fan low or loud? Are the seats on a gradient? Rarely, if ever, should the layout make or break your performance (or your decision to speak) but a key part of your preparation involves understanding your surroundings and using these to your advantage. At a minimum, request photos of the premises.

While organisers might chuckle at your queries, experienced ones will appreciate the care you commit to your craft.

Second, where possible, visit the space beforehand. Acoustics vary from room to room and may influence your need for a mic. Bright lights pointed in your direction could make it difficult for you to make eye contact with your audience. A few years back, I delivered a talk to the British Council in Singapore. They held it in the Old Parliament Building, a colonial style landmark established during the heyday of British imperialism. It thrilled me. Rarely am I afforded the privilege of lecturing in such a beautiful hall, its dubious origins notwithstanding. Being in Singapore, natural light flooded the room and enough frosty air to comfort a polar bear. I ran two laps around the building beforehand to keep warm during the speech. While the hall was beautiful in every way, there were plenty of shortcomings: the old wooden floors creaked when I walked; while some audience members sat near the front, others opted for the very back, placing roughly 40-50 metres between them and me; they offered me a handheld mic; and the natural light meant that the photographs I displayed were barely visible. Happily, images of the venue are abundant online—you can search it now and see for yourself—so I could recognise these potential problems early on and plan accordingly.

If you are on an international speaking tour, scouting visits are near impossible. In those instances, pose as many questions as you can and dig around online for visuals. We feel much more confident when walking into a room familiar to us.

My third suggestion is to arrive at the site early. Knowing the layout is essential in gauging the prospective number of attendees and planning your movement within the room. However, the key reason for arriving early is to modify it to your advantage. Depending on the type of speaker you are, you will either stand fixed at the front of the room or rove freely. Is this possible in the room assigned? What if you move around some items? I recall interviewing for my first academic job at the University of Auckland. Academic interviews involve two stages: a seminar delivered to the faculty and an interview with a hiring committee. As I arrived a day in advance, I visited the lecture theatre identified in the invitation. What I found was troubling.

I walked into a moderately sized theatre that could accommodate some 75 students. Seats and tables were in a trapezoid shape. At the front was a table and a separate computer console. All of this is standard. What made the site awkward was everything else. Someone placed a desktop lectern on the right side of the desk. To the left of it was the computer console and flanked by a broken overhead projector. To the right was a wall. A rubbish bin stood to the left of the desk. Finally, text about some discrete element of tort law adorned the blackboard.

Two consequences of this setup troubled me. First, the apparatuses combined to conceal three-quarters of the speaker. While some may think this trivial (maybe advantageous), the consequences are significant. Imagine yourself at the theatre and a column obstructs your view of the principal actor. Craning our necks just to see the performance distracts, irritates, and eventually exasperates us. Second, the speaker looks small, which is never to your advantage. For those who have seen an NBA match, notice how imposing the players are. Because of their size, it is impossible for us to take our eyes off them. Third, the obstructions neutralise the impact of a speaker's gestures, clothes, and overall presence. Since 90% of communication is non-verbal, by standing behind obstructions we render our performance that much more difficult to connect with. This meant that the set-up would hurt my chances of landing the position.

I quickly went to work. I moved the rubbish bin to the rear corner of the room. Besides being an eyesore, you do not want to be associated with trash. Next, I took the overhead projector out of the room. This minor act de-cluttered the table. I placed the lectern on the far left end of the desk, pointing it towards the audience at a 45-degree angle. So positioned, the speaker (me) was now the centre of the room, in full view of the audience, and with easy access to my materials. With these slight adjustments, I made myself the focal point, allowing them to appreciate my outfit and hand gestures. Finally, I wiped down the blackboard with a brush. As it still looked untidy, I wet some serviettes and cleaned it a second time. I interviewed out of term so banked on the room being used for the seminars only. Taken individually, each change sounds minor, even juvenile. Taken together, the change was dramatic. The next day, I stood at the centre of the room and greeted every (future) colleague as they entered the room. In fact, so pronounced was the change that one professor smiled slyly and remarked: 'looks a little different'. It sure did and while I do not credit this with landing me the job and launching my academic career, it helped me leave a positive impression.

*

I just hinted at the other advantage of arriving early: gauging and meeting the audience. By being on the ground beforehand, you can observe everyone trickle in. You should smile, mouth a polite hello, and even strike up small talk with the audience members closest to you. These minor acts will endear you to members of the audience. Having established a connection, eye contact is easier. Their nodding will be more enthusiastic, and they will forgive jokes that go awry. By arriving early, you have an opportunity to convert attendees into allies, bolstering your position in front of the rest. Do the same with a fresh set of attendees during the intervals. Incidentally, if small talk makes you uncomfortable, stay at the front and review your notes, while looking up as people trickle in. Again, you gain important intelligence by observing your audience beforehand (more on audiences in chapters 8 and 14) while also making yourself appear more committed. I would avoid frantic paper-shuffling or note-taking lest you appear ill-prepared.

*

My penultimate remark about space pertains to your movement within it. Having arrived early, practice your walking route. To be blunt, never mimic a tree. Movement is your friend as it a) brings you closer to the audience and b) makes your delivery more dynamic. While waiting for your talk to begin, casually practice movements and routes: stepping from behind the lectern, walking alongside the blackboard, or approaching the front row. Gauge which movements feel natural and which feel awkward. Repeat them until they sink in. The pre-talk stroll will boost the probability of even uncomfortable walkers making better use of their space.

*

I conclude with an overall observation about space and how it can make us feel. Observe your surroundings. Are you in a cafe, office, or library? What do these surroundings communicate to you? Do they make you feel confident or vulnerable? An environment can inspire us or drain our presence altogether. When I attended a football match at the Camp Nou, for example, I felt enlivened both by the spirit of football and of Messi.

What always impresses me about Messi is the paradox of his personality. On the pitch, his demeanour is nonchalant, self-assured, and even a little irreverent. In an interview he is the opposite, appearing afraid, awkward, and dull. It is easy to chalk this to his proficiency in football. The magic man is magisterial on a pitch. But what about the studio? Must he—and we—always suffer? If I coached Messi on public speaking, I would tell him to visualise the pitch during his interviews. Imagine yourself strolling up and down the field, stalking an opportunity. Imagine yourself receiving a pass and then exploding into the opponent's half, dribbling past a stunned midfield. Imagine yourself jinking a defender before laying the ball in the path of your teammates. And finally, imagine the satisfaction you feel as your teammates hoist you up to celebrate another victory.

Wherever you speak, do what you can to appropriate the space in this way. Visualise a place in which you feel powerful, creative and inspired. I never lecture in a lecture theatre; I am in the courtroom, the ring, the desert, the forest, or a Greek agora. These spaces fill me with confidence, enabling me to feel better about my surroundings and more positive when delivering my speech.

Once the curtains open, the floor is yours.

7

THE AUDIENCE

We have arrived at the last chapter of the preparatory phase. Before I go on, I repeat my earlier point about the interconnectedness of these sections. Space, speaker, and speech are essential elements to reflect upon when producing a public speaking event. While many amateur speakers rate the speech highest in importance, the previous chapters have forewarned you to the danger of that assumption. Poor acoustics can wreck your talk as quickly as poor movement, irrespective of the quality of the content you present.

I favoured space, speaker, and speech in my discussion as you have significant sway over them. While there are limitations, there are plenty of ways to exploit these to your advantage. From playing introductory music to locating your lectern, from adjusting your arm movements to studying an Eldredge knot, from reducing adverbs to planting well-timed gags, you can finesse most aspects of your performance, strengthening your ability to be captivating and memorable.

My last point about preparation applies to the audience for there is no speech without one. Eventually, you will realise that the audience is more important than everything else. A delighted audience can steer you to the heavens just as a disappointed one will fire up the furnaces. So important is the audience, I devote one of my advanced skills chapters (Chapter 13) to the topic. Before venturing into the advanced techniques, you would be wise to include the audience to your preparation programme. What does this mean?

Speakers treat audiences as the great unknown. This is sensible. Irrespective of the talk you present, you won't recognise the vast majority of the people in attendance. Worse, their politics, partialities, and personalities will remain anonymous throughout the event and, almost assuredly, afterwards. You may extract something about them from their interactions with you, chiefly the questions they propose. Beyond these unpredictable and inconsistent interventions, they remain nameless. Under these circumstances, is preparation advisable or even possible? The answer is a resounding yes. Over the years, I developed three techniques to aid me in preparing for the audience. Each of these will help you prepare for most audience-driven challenges.

PREDICTIONS

The first approach involves predicting your audience's composition. You can presage the public likely to attend your talk from the organisers, promotions, and platforms. To apply an easy example, the New Zealand Chamber of Commerce invited me to speak on the market for transnational education. They wished to hear about my experience with Australian universities operating in Malaysia. Was this a viable sector for Kiwi educational service providers? I could immediately envision the size of the audience (small), the profile (executives with a background in private education), and the politics (politically liberal, fiscally conservative, and personally entrepreneurial). With information in hand, I adjusted my speech to deliver a performance that would resonate with a small, expert, and assertive audience. Five minutes on the Chamber's webpage and I was already better positioned to deliver a more effective talk.

Predictions are risky business. However, with a little practice, you will learn to assess probabilities rather than to make predictions. Also, once your reputation precedes you, your audiences will self-select, simplifying your task. This is inevitable, hence the invitations we receive: organisers don't build events around speakers unfamiliar to them. It's too perilous. Even when your topic changes, the crowd will reproduce itself. You entice the attendees as much as your topics do. The better you understand yourself, the more capable you are at predicting your audience.

THE CHOIR, THE CURMUDGEON, AND THE EXPLORER

The second approach requires more effort but pays greater dividends. It also involves prediction, but you cast the net wider. You should predict the different subgroups with an interest in your topic and account for them in your speech. For example, I often use introductions to highlight the groups most curious about the topic. I then commit to satisfying some, all, or none of them. My preference is to satisfy a few, while excluding others. This practice is less adversarial than it sounds.

In almost any talk, you will face three types: the choir, curmudgeons, and explorers. The choir represents the attendees favourable to your position, open to being persuaded by your position, or sympathetic to you as a person. Since they already support you or your position, you need only provide them with what they came for: you. You should adopt a mind-set of acknowledgement, appreciation, and gratitude in relation to them when drawing up your speech. While this may sound Machiavellian, they are your base: nurture them.

Next is the curmudgeon. Imagine yourself in the pits of hell because that is where the curmudgeon wishes you were and will send you at the first chance. We are dealing with the same three variations as the choir: those who disagree with you, those predisposed to disagreeing with you, and those sceptical of you. With this group, your aim is to minimise their disruptive potential. In the same way that comedians prepare for hecklers, prepare for curmudgeons (incidentally, watching comedians handle hecklers is great practice and splendid fun). In my introductions, I acknowledge the curmudgeon, identifying their particular grievance in a self-serving tone. The acknowledgement will placate some curmudgeons but is more useful in augmenting your credibility with the rest of your audience. You appear aware and magnanimous and become more likeable. Sometimes, however, when politics are personal, I call them out when the disruption begins. With the confrontational approach, my aims are to (a) put the curmudgeon on notice that I will take no prisoners and (b) conscript the choir to my flanks. I use military metaphors to convey the antagonist disposition of this group. You are not Dr Martin Luther King and will not win them over. You should prepare yourself for a skirmish.

Last, we find the explorer. This group comprises individuals who have no vested interests, at least none that they recognise. They wish to understand more about the topic or speaker. Think not of Christopher Columbus who coveted treasure but of Ibn Battuta who searched for knowledge and encounters. Explorers are sincere, curious, and affable. I caution you, however, not to underestimate them. Almost all explorers are erudite; you may even encounter a few polymaths along the way. I urge caution as they pose questions neither to aid nor to sink. Pure enquiry motivates them as they feel no allegiance to you or your cause. When we include to this predisposition their strength of intellect, expect searching questions.

Though this may seem counterintuitive, the explorer is more dangerous than the curmudgeon. You can see the curmudgeon coming at a distance and they have little standing with your supporters to begin with. Irrespective of the blows that rain down on you, your credibility will remain intact. In contrast, explorers pose robust questions and audiences expect equally robust answers. You must understand most aspects of your speech and be capable of navigating through enquiries you did not foresee. Above all, however, avoid getting into a duel of wits with the explorer: first, they are not antagonistic like the curmudgeon and, second, they can best you. Irrespective of their intellect, always remember that you are the expert on your speech and thus always in the stronger position.

In most instances, this trinity will shape your audience. Proportional representation of each group, however, varies. By developing your abilities to recognise and engage with each group, you are ready to deal with whoever walks through the door.

WORST-CASE SCENARIO

I use my last approach as a catch-all. Everyone has rough days: perhaps our voice, appearance, or even cognition feels off-kilter. Perhaps all of them do. This is a wretched time to deliver a public performance and yet deliver you must if it is speech day. You can deal with rough days, and I outline tactics in Chapter 16. For now, I conclude with remarks about rough days provoked by poor audiences.

When I worked as a barrister, my mentor always proclaimed that there is no such thing as a poor judge or a bad jury. There are judges and juries unmoved by bad barristers. Years later and I still hear echoes of this point. I also recycle his lesson, recently declaring that poor students are the product of bad teaching. Are there poor judges and bad juries (and poor students)? There are! Some judges are vainglorious. Many juries don't pay attention. Some students don't give a toss. With these individuals, we must double our efforts, persuading them to listen first before trying to convince them of the argument. Regardless of how bad you believe your audience to be, you must still try to win them over.

Similarly, expert public speakers take responsibility. We never blame the audience. Our ambition is to perform well irrespective of the people seated in front of us. What does this mean from a preparatory and pragmatic perspective? First, that you must know yourself and second, that you must prepare for the worst-case scenario.

I have already spoken at length about the relevance of your motivation and personality when preparing for a public performance. One important characteristic that I left out is the preference you feel for an audience of a particular persuasion. To use myself as an example, I perform best with audiences that are slightly sceptical. I enjoy the challenge of building a persuasive argument and trialling it by fire. I also revel in skirmishes, so a little controversy does not go amiss either. Finally, manifestations of exuberance by the audience are my drug of choice. Give me a rambunctious and animated audience and you've made my day.

This is not the same for others. Many of my colleagues, especially members of the British Bar, bench, and academy, prefer the opposite, valuing demur and sober crowds. My Swedish counterparts prefer non-confrontational ones. My Eastern background blends with my Western upbringing, resulting in my penchant for organised chaos. By now, it should be obvious which audiences bemuse me. To be blunt, audiences that prefer stoicism to stimulation are the bane of my existence as a public speaker.

What does this tell us? Simple: like you and others, I respond to the surrounding circumstances, irrespective of the confidence and experience I possess. Knowing yourself means knowing the audience types you prefer and the audience types you suffer. Since you will suffer many of your audiences, prepare a strategy for worst-case scenarios. You should alternate between two approaches when dealing with difficult audiences. Just as you will not win over the curmudgeon, you will not sway a poor audience. You thus have little cause to prepare anything more than perfunctory strategies. When confronted by a difficult audience, I adopt one of two strategies: the mirror or the sparring session.

The mirror is my first port of call. Having logged countless hours practicing before a mirror, I revert to this mindset. Like when practicing before the mirror, I worry not how a difficult audience perceives me. The mirror allows me to tune them out. They will watch the performance I've delivered umpteen times before. By visualizing a mirror instead of the audience, I can use my preparation to drown out the unfortunate ambiance.

The second strategy is bolder. Here I use the opportunity afforded to trial a new speaking technique. In the same way that boxers use sparring sessions to rehearse skills, I use bad audiences to practice something new. Like the mirror approach, even astute audiences are unlikely to pick up on what I am doing. Whether the sparring session pertains to my command of space, speech, or myself matters not. Continue with the talk that you prepared but introduce a new technique under development. A difficult audience is an excellent occasion to take part in a live-fire exercise. Incidentally, it is advisable to always have a list of skills you wish to develop. My list helps me plan my professional development.

I conclude this section with two warnings. First, the mirror and the sparring session are useful strategies as the natural reaction for a speaker when faced with a difficult audience—myself included—is to try to win them over. Sadly, the only thing worse than a difficult audience is a desperate speaker. Since you will fail, do not bother. Instead, use your skills to get through the occasion while exerting the least energy and suffering only minimal pain. Second, resist the temptation to fluff your speech. Even if you aren't connecting with the audience, even if they're contemptuous of you, a terrible performance reflects poorly on you. The audience has the privilege of being anonymous and thus walking away with their reputations intact. You do not have that luxury. Your audiences must know you as the speaker who delivers, even under trying circumstances, rather than the one who tantrums.

*

A key element in our quest to become captivating and memorable is the audience. There are ways to nurture them, just as there are an equal number of ways to alienate them. Beyond these brief tips, there is much more you can do with the audience to enhance the quality of your performance. For those eager to learn more, you may skip ahead to Chapter 13.

PART 2: BASIC SKILLS

INTRODUCTION

Effective public speakers balance technique, skill, and art. Each element thus applies to your development. The distinction is simple but vital, and I encourage you to think of public speaking through this trinity. Techniques are practices that facilitate the action. You should treat them as the rules of the game. Skill is the level of proficiency you possess in applying the techniques and, thus, in performing. This element comprises the dedication and discipline you commit to learning the rules and improving your application. Art is the mystery ingredient.

This book is about public speaking techniques. I signpost pathways to developing your skill throughout and try to provoke reflection about your artistic contribution. Techniques, however, remain the book's backbone and purpose.

I subdivide techniques into levels of difficulty and, ultimately, levels of proficiency. There are only two differences between an amateur and a master: the master knows more techniques and is more proficient at their application than the amateur. When learning an unknown practice, it is best to begin with the basics. For all the popularity of 'sink or swim' bravado, a child will drown if you throw them in at the deep end before teaching them the dog paddle.

In the following section, I outline five basic techniques: the narrative, mind-mapping, tone, tempo, and movement. The first two techniques pertain to speech, the second and third are about the speaker, and the last one targets space. This builds on some lessons I covered in the previous chapters, which are also relevant to what you should practice. The one outstanding element of public speaking—audience—factors into advanced techniques detailed in the final section. Learning these skills and developing proficiency will set you apart from most other public speakers, not because of the array of techniques you will know and the skills you will possess—though these matter—but principally because of the literacy you will gain in public speaking.

I conclude my introductory remarks with a few words about the elephant in the room—art—which I explain with a football anecdote.

My opening paragraph was deliberately left open: what is the mystery ingredient and how do we get it? Let us reflect on two of the greatest football players to have ever played the game: Lionel Messi and Cristiano Ronaldo. Statistically, it is difficult to find athletes who have dominated a sport more than they have. Simone Biles, Jessica Ennis-Hill, Roger Federer, Lewis Hamilton, Serena Williams, and Tiger Woods are once in a generation athletes in their respective sports. But, if we factor in the sheer number of competitors, they do not come close to Messi and Ronaldo. In the aggregate, how many people play tennis or drive Formula 1 cars? Whatever the number, it is infinitesimally smaller than the number of people who play football, underscoring the level of dominance these two phenomena have achieved.

Between Messi and Ronaldo, who is the very best? The debate will never end, for there is no legitimate measure against which we can compare them. I admire the prowess of both, but neither of their personalities (Ronaldo is too extroverted and Messi is too introverted). While I respect both, it is for varied reasons. Football fans know that Ronaldo is a machine: epic speed and strength combine with an ability to dribble that has yielded championships across a range of tournaments. Less well known is Ronaldo's dedication to maintaining that epic speed and strength. In a radio interview, Carlos Tevez spoke both glowingly and bitterly about Ronaldo's 6am free-kick sessions. As a fellow masochist, I admire his commitment to fitness.

Anyone who knows football knows that Messi is different. He is also a bullet on the pitch and can dribble his way through a herd of gazelles. He has scored a near equal number of goals to the number of matches he has played—and he has played a staggering number of matches—without being a striker. But he performs every goal, run, dribble, pass, and free-kick with a bizarre form of effortlessness, often leaving the viewer with the impression that he just walked the ball into the net and his team to victory. Messi may be the furthest thing from nonchalant, but his ability to appear so when scoring hundreds of goals is the artistry that many others and I admire about him.

Art is always a secret ingredient. Personality plays a part as does a little passion, but the X factor will forever remain a mystery. Try as we do to classify it, to explain it, and even to rate it, some secrets will remain just that.

I can teach you techniques that will help you improve your public speaking skills and I can teach you how to practice them to ensure that you become a skilled speaker. What I cannot do is teach you to be you: that is the window through which art enters the room.

8

NARRATIVE STORYTELLING

Ted Talks are popular. Despite emerging well over a decade ago, it remains a tour de force. In an era of goldfish, its enduring character is a testament to humanity's intrinsic desire to teach, to learn, and to entertain!

So popular is Ted, that it has spawned an entire ecosystem, including countless books, videos, and podcasts on the Ted phenomenon. Personally, I have attended several Ted events, always as a spectator, and it remains a personal goal to speak at their flagship conference. It will thus not surprise you to learn that I am an avid consumer of books relating to Ted, engaging closely with the ones on public speaking. What makes Ted so popular? Look above at the title of this chapter.

This claim is not without its detractors. Critics lament the format, the audience, the social capital of the speakers, and many other features of Ted. I am not convinced by the denunciations. It would be difficult, if not impossible, to organise thousands of public speaking events if the organisers had not cracked some magical code. While the level of success Ted enjoys is impressive, it is not magic that keeps people engaged. Rather, the answer is as ancient as humanity. Ted Talks tell stories, stories that are both captivating and memorable.

During a single day, we are likely to hear dozens if not hundreds of stories. We overhear them when sitting on a bus or in a cafe ('after X did this, Y did that'). We watch them in programmes and in films. We read them in books and, depending on the quality of the journalist, in newspapers. We recognise them in an Instagram feed. And we tell them ourselves. Much of our communication happens in storytelling format. This is hardly surprising since biology and fate book-end our lives in stories: parents tell their children stories from a young age and, upon our passing, our familiars share stories about our lives (or so we hope!).

Despite the prevalence of stories in our lives, many public speakers eschew the storytelling model and, instead, pursue the content format. They build their speech around a series of facts: facts about the policies their party will adopt, facts about the product they are trying to sell, or facts about the contract the other side broke, to name a few I heard in the week when writing this chapter. The only reason I even remember these topics is because I jotted them down in my notes. As part of my fieldwork for this chapter, I attended several talks to determine how popular the storytelling model is in public speaking events. The answer: not nearly as popular as it should be.

Many years ago, I discovered the world's worst kept secret: humans like stories. What would happen if instead of making arguments in courtrooms or delivering lectures to students, I told them stories about the topic? The answer: I become captivating and memorable. Stories are hypnotic, making it the easiest way to connect with people of different persuasions, politics, and personalities. The storytelling structure is a format that speaks to all of us.

What does a story include? Just as there is no magic to stories, there is scant mystery to their components. First, stories develop around protagonists, whether pleasant or hateful and often both. Second, the plots of stories develop linearly with subsequent incidents building upon previous ones. Third, controversy abounds: protagonists may live or die (do not grow attached to any Game of Thrones characters) and happenings are banal or unexpected (paradoxically, M. Night Shyamalan has made the unexpected banal). Fourth, they subject the listener to a rollercoaster of emotions. Fifth, a crescendo will always conclude the story.

Each component is essential: a story that cannot deliver them is no story at all. In the rest of this chapter, I explain how you can use each component to develop a very successful format for structuring your speeches.

PROTAGONISTS

While each component is essential, the protagonist remains primordial. In literary terms, we understand the protagonist as the leading character. For our purposes, however, classify any character essential to your story as a protagonist: this can include casual or supporting characters as well.

Protagonists serve a variety of purposes. Foremost, however, is their role in connecting you to the audience and eliciting a particular reaction. For example, while a story about Donald Trump is likely to trigger most audiences, for too many reasons to name, the emotions he provokes are hardly to your advantage. Trump is most often associated with anger (rage even), petulance, megalomania, and in the best scenarios, pity. While these emotions have their place, you play a risky game if you lead with them as you have begun your speech by boiling the blood of your audience. Once our blood pressure rises, our ability to focus erodes, placing the speaker at a disadvantage. You should thus avoid leading with controversial characters.

You would be mistaken in assuming that this means you should choose a bland protagonist to open with. Blandness is by definition forgettable and, yet again, elicits the wrong feelings. The lesson is to avoid extremes and to choose characters or, more accurately, personality types that the audience can easily associate with the thrust of your story and of your wider speech.

Let's play a game. I will name individuals and link them to popular perceptions. I have selected individuals known to most but research those you do not recognise to appreciate the characteristics I identify.

George Clooney: dapper, sophisticated, and suave
Alexandra Ocasio-Cortez: committed, expressive, and progressive
Emmanuel Macron: articulate, educated, and hypocritical
Nelson Mandela: devoted, gregarious, and resilient
Oprah Winfrey: entrepreneurial, influential, and intelligent

We associate each protagonist with a different narrative. To use a facile example, it makes little sense to build a story about the changing nature of Hollywood around Ocasio-Cortez. Obviously, either Clooney or Winfrey would be more useful here in the same way that Ocasio-Cortez is better suited for a story about youth or even misogyny in modern politics. Key is selecting someone who relates to the story you will tell. Alternatively, you can develop a fictitious character that meets your criteria or, when in doubt, use yourself. Personal narratives are reliable for we know our experiences best of all and, when in doubt, we can fabricate the arcs.

To be certain of your choice, poll a few people about the protagonist and test their response. If your protagonist elicits the emotions you are targeting, move on to your plot. If they do not, rethink the protagonist.

PLOT PROGRESSION

Plot is the second most important element in the narrative. It is the story itself! Just as a boring protagonist will not win you any friends, a boring story will lose you plenty. I say more about developing a story in the next three subsections: controversy, emotions, and crescendo are key to telling a captivating and memorable tale. For now, however, I share a few general remarks about storytelling.

First, unlike with cinema or literature where mysteries and cliffhangers are the norm, in public speaking the opposite is true:

audiences much prefer the comfort of predictability. This sounds counterintuitive: what better way to keep the audience enthralled than building up to the big reveal? Not so. Recall what I wrote in Chapter 6: listening to public speakers is exhausting. Irrespective of the speaker, audiences will drift in and out. They are also anxious about missing key information. None of this works to your advantage. You will notice the tension and become anxious yourself. Yet there is a simple way of countering these tendencies: be predictable and open with your conclusion.

I enjoy spaghetti westerns. There are plenty of aspects that appeal to me, including the predictability of the plot line: we know how the story will end. Somebody will shoot the protagonist we are warming up to; the cute little boy playing in the road dies in cross-fire; and, by the film's end, the Magnificent Seven collapse into the Bedraggled Three. Contrast this film genre with HBO programmes such as The Wire or Game of Thrones. These days, we count our blessings when the characters we adore survive for another season or even just one more episode. Uncertainty fuels these shows, with their writers creating unending anxiety for viewers. For public speakers, anxiety works against you as it disrupts both concentration and memory. Predictability helps the audience to keep track of what you're saying; you do them a disservice by serving up a mystery or a guessing game. Move at pace and predictably: your audiences will love you for it.

Opening with the conclusion is a common practice for barristers. By leading with your argument or thesis and then working backwards, the judge understands what you will evidence. They can then focus on the quality of the argument and supporting documents rather than trying to figure out your general position. This is also common practice for professors or should be. Lead with 'lessons' students should take away from the lecture. By noting these at the outset, they see all the information through a defined prism. By knowing what they should learn, we minimise their anxiety about missing the takeaways of the day. To reiterate potent emotions such as anxiety disrupt focus.

To the chagrin of a Singaporean audience—and to mine in due course—following what I thought was a riveting 60 minute lecture on inequality, one audience member (an Explorer - see Chapter 8) posed a question that sank my speech: 'this was very interesting but what exactly are you arguing for?' Neither they nor their question was malicious. I had just failed to outline the message. This question was on their mind throughout, meaning they missed most of what I said. Outlining your argument straight away will ensure that your audience listens to you rather than struggles over your message.

A third remark about stories is that they need not be elaborate: simple is best. While I am not encouraging the simplicity of a picture book, even this would be preferable to the labyrinthine sagas we make audiences suffer. I cannot stress this enough, hence my earlier suggestion to shave 20% of your final draft: less is more accessible. To be clear, it is not only a matter of excessive content. Rather, it is in the details of the story and the links your audience must draw between them. For example, consider Tolkien's masterpiece: the Lord of the Rings. A true philologist, we celebrate Tolkien for the exquisite prose of the trilogy, not to mention the richness of the characters, descriptions, and plot line. The trilogy is also bloated beyond recognition and fans have produced texts that explain storylines lost on all except the most rigorous readers. Your audience will not have the patience, the ability, nor the interest in labouring to listen. Your speech must therefore be simple enough for them to understand with minimal effort. Once they descend into 'deciphering' your words, you have lost them.

To ensure that my storylines are simple, I use two techniques to develop and organise the information: the mind map and the illustration. So important is the mind map, I dedicate Chapter 9 to it so I will not provide more than an overview here.

Mind maps are a useful tool for organising information relationally. What do I mean? Imagine the most common instruments used when planning a speech: lecture notes, overhead slides, and scripts. Each represents information linearly. Much like reading a book, we proceed sequentially from one page to the next. Speakers and listeners perceive the topic in a unidirectional manner. We fix a trajectory and events move forward towards an end point. But is a linear trajectory a useful way of thinking of the 'evolution' of the Beatles' music? Do sports teams develop linearly? What about scientific discovery or even learning: does one step always lead to another? Information does not exist linearly even if we can represent it in this form.

In contrast, mind maps represent information relationally. Instead, we see the variables alongside one another. Mind maps present information holistically rather than sequentially, providing us with a unique way of relating to it, interpreting it, and articulating it. Mind maps force a break with the misleading format that dominates speeches, allowing for far greater adaptability and malleability. Imagine studying Rembrandt. If he were alive, would the best way of learning from the master involve repeating his brush strokes? This is an inane way of understanding his painting style. Instead, we take a big picture view before breaking down the many elements and engaging with them relationally. His muse influences the colour schema, the materials selected, and his many acts of layering. Each variable affects the others. Slides home in on trees; mind maps capture forests.

My second technique to simplify storylines is the illustration. Just as images inspired Rembrandt, so too should your speech be communicable visually. If you can see it, you can develop it into the message that guides your audience. For example, in a speech I delivered on Brexit — the United Kingdom's withdrawal from the European Union — and trade policy, I imagined British rowers paddling the British Isles further from the European continent and settling in the centre of the Atlantic ocean. This image captured the two messages I wish to convey to the audience. First, the widening distance between the two lands means the ties between them will wither. Second, the UK will find itself closer to American shores but still quite a way off. By associating my speeches with visual representations, both imaginary and real, I am better placed to present the information. I need only describe to the audience the image, what it conveys, and why I illustrated it in this manner to deliver an engrossing speech.

By allowing predictability to inform the structure and delivery of your narrative, you will, ironically, produce more captivating and memorable talks. Your audience will not squander time, patience, or energy. Knowing how the story will conclude your audience to focus on the elements you want them to pay attention to: your message and the action you aim to inspire.

CONTROVERSY

Controversy is key to any story. Contrary to its use in popular parlance, controversy is not always negative, at least not in a narrative. Rather, it is a useful literary device when advancing a story. It creates a point of debate and deliberation, encouraging the audience to focus. Returning to my statistics from Chapter 1, recall that listeners only keep 10% of what they hear, in contrast to 40-60% of what they engage in. By using controversy to create moments of reflection, even a monologue can instigate concentration. Without controversy, a speech is nothing more than raw information, easily forgotten.

I use an old American adage to centre controversy's value: where's the beef? At key moments of your speech, ask yourself this question and you will pinpoint the controversial elements. For example, in a recent lecture on the China-USA trade war, I began with a controversial statement (which doubled as my conclusion): trade wars are inevitable, for conflict is perpetual in the global economy.

Now ask yourself: where's the beef? There are at least two, and more likely three points of controversy in my conclusion:

    1. Trade wars are inevitable,

    2. conflict is perpetual, and

    3. cooperation is anomalous in the global economy.

I dedicated much of my talk to explaining and substantiating these three claims. By beginning from an unconventional starting point, I sparked my audience's curiosity. By navigating between controversies, I sustained the audience's attention throughout the speech. Stated otherwise, controversy stimulates the listener: they understand that both the issues and your claims are contentious, and their focus should be on understanding your arguments and testing your evidence. You've already signposted the conclusion so there is nothing to figure out.

Essential here is a point I highlight in Chapter 2 and elaborate upon here. Public speaking is an act of persuasion and not of truth giving or truth seeking. Let me explain. I recently encountered a small club of public speakers whom I would describe as eccentric. Members of this club, or movement perhaps, allege that both speaker and audience are truth-seekers, allied in their desire to understand one another. Instead of 'playing the audience' with performances and techniques—they discourage many from the practices I promote in this book—a speaker should share themselves and their truth (the phrase 'be vulnerable' comes up often). Despite the flippancy of my tone, I understand their aim: to promote authenticity. You might recall from Chapter 6 that I encourage in-depth research and discourage all forms of fabrication. You can get away with embellishing while the tactical use of hyperbole has its place as well. Still, you should never deceive and always speak authentically. I differ on what we are being authentic about. Sometimes audiences wish to know the speaker: political rallies are a perfect example. But to suggest that personal authenticity is what the audience wishes for misrepresents the purpose of oration.

At the heart of most public speaking is persuasion. I do not mean that all audiences are like judges or juries. Rather, in every performance, the audience is testing your argument and asking themselves if they find it persuasive. Consider it this way, which of the following phrases are you least likely to hear after a public talk:

- What a powerful speaker!
- Man, that was boring.
- What was her argument about...?
- I'm convinced.
- I couldn't really follow them; they were all over the place.
- The speaker's truth moved me. I feel like I really know them.

The answer is self-evident. As explained in Chapter 5, audiences judge public speakers on their performance. It is rare for audiences to disbelieve the speaker (to distrust them is another matter). The issue is not whether the speaker is telling the truth but whether the speaker's truth is convincing to the audience. At some point, you have heard or will hear a listener say that the speaker's 'heart just wasn't in it'. They use this phrase not when they think a speaker is being disingenuous, but when they are unconvinced by what the speaker says. That feeling is especially acute when they doubt the speaker's conviction.

Once we accept that persuasion is the art and name of the game, the dynamics change. You will no longer see yourself as a conduit to or interlocutor of information, but a participant shaping the narrative. By adding controversy to your narrative, you make it more captivating; by providing a resolution to the controversy, you render it memorable; and, by identifying—even creating—the controversy, you set the parameters of the story. If these parameters prove lacklustre or do not convince, you can change them.

EMOTIONS

We expect stories to elicit emotions. We read books or watch movies for this very reason. To an extent, we are all experts in emotions. We can distinguish between feelings such as happiness, sadness, elation, exhilaration, and rage, just as we know which actions will trigger each of them. While we are experts in identifying and feeling emotions, most public speakers are less competent at using emotions to their advantage.

Speakers tend not to think of emotions instrumentally or, if they do, feel guilty about the prospect of manipulating the emotions of someone else. While I appreciate the reservations, we do ourselves a disservice by disregarding them. Emotions are expressions of our humanity that facilitate the forging of connections, for emotions are reciprocal: we feel emotions more deeply when experiencing them with others. A moment of happiness can quickly burst into ecstasy when we experience it with another. Likewise, the tears of a loved one make us cry as well. Audiences often mirror back the emotions the speaker conveys.

Which emotions should you convey and elicit? Circumstances arc vital when answering this question. There are some simple decisions, however. In all circumstances, you must project enthusiasm. If you are not excited about the occasion, your audience will sense your boredom and reflect it back to you tenfold. Equally, you must also convey gratitude to the audience. They could use their time otherwise, but they are listening to you. The least you can do is express your appreciation.

Just as some emotions are essential, we must keep others in check. Frustration is the first no-no. While rage induced by the topic is perfectly acceptable—when giving a lecture on child poverty, I felt so infuriated that I accidentally broke the lectern microphone—frustration with the audience is not. The instant the audience feels your frustration towards them—for example, for failing to answer a question or for becoming distracted—they will shut down and even become contemptuous of you. Frustration will wreck your rapport with the audience at breakneck speed. Another emotion to avoid is disappointment, whether regarding the turnout, the tone, the lack of engagement, the lack of knowledge, or anything else you notice about the occasion or audience. Academics, for example, are especially sensitive to a lack of engagement. They become disappointed, even dejected and communicate this to their students overtly and implicitly. It never works. Students do not feel more motivated, engaged, or committed, the worse the professor treats them. Quite the opposite, you demoralise them further, ensuring that you waste your time together.

Not expressing negative emotions is far more difficult than sharing positive ones. Return to my opening paragraph: emotions are human. We feel them and our faces reveal our feelings. Concealing these is neither easy nor desirable, which is why I return to the very point I made earlier about audiences. Before and during a performance, remind yourself that the audience has a tough task. They are anxious about not understanding something or, worse, not knowing what they should try to understand. They will experience lapses in attention and fatigue, both of which will cause them to lose the thread. And they will get bored. The task you prepared for is effortless in comparison!

I caution speakers against expecting too much of their audiences. In the best instances, they will be engaged, asking and answering questions freely. They will laugh at your jokes and reward you with feelings of fulfilment and success. In the worst instances, you will feel the life slowly seeping out of you. Not only will they not laugh at your jokes, they will also shoot some of the most patronising, condescending, and brutal expressions your way. Your confidence and self-esteem will beeline for the door. Regardless of which audience you face, your speech must remain steady. Under no circumstances should you let your emotions run away from you. You must resist feeling frustrated or disappointed with your audience. Instead, follow the techniques I identify in Chapter 16 to reel back an audience that is slipping away.

Treat their disengagement not as a personal slight but as a tactical opportunity to revisit your strategy.

CRESCENDO

Crescendo is my favourite word. It describes climaxes and culminations in musical arrangements, an attempt at reaching the heavens before we glide (or crash) back to earth. You know a crescendo when you hear one: we are calm afterwards. It is my favourite word for I adore that the sound mirrors the meaning.

Just as I enjoy music that follows this pattern—I am listening to the collaboration between Metropole Orkest and Basement Jaxx and Ramin Djawadi's Night King as I write this section of the chapter—I also enjoy stories that exhibit crescendos. Many authors use the crescendo device to bring their story to a conclusion. Some obvious ones include Rowling's Harry Potter series, Tolkien's Lord of the Rings, and Haley's Autobiography of Malcolm X (though Haley was a master of the stealth crescendo, a far more advanced skill).

Crescendos are also an effective device in public speaking. Just as the controversy hooks your audience, the crescendo releases them, facilitating a smooth transition to your recap and concluding statement. Before I explain how to use the crescendo, I should emphasise that effective crescendos are more scalpel than sledgehammer, more Tim Burton than Michael Bay. Big, loud exploding things may seem like a crescendo but they are nothing more than big, loud exploding things. The skill of the crescendo is the subtlety with which we deliver it. We do not conceal it nor does it sneak up on you; that would fall foul of the need for a predictable plot line. We do it with finesse, ensuring that the audience feels it as it rises and releases. Michael Bay (think Transformers) uses lots of explosions to distract from his contrived plot lines. Killing the nemesis with an explosion also kills the story. Burton, in contrast, and to a lesser extent Spike Lee and Francis Ford Coppola, savour the crescendo, treating it as a final farewell. For the listener, the crescendo produces a sigh of relief. For the speaker, it is a sigh of success. An effective crescendo is memorable. Think of Michael Corleone ordering an orgy of assassinations in the Godfather and how it instantly implants itself in your memory, obscuring everything else.

How do we design an effective crescendo? Having already told your audience the conclusion, you cannot surprise them by killing off a protagonist out of the blue. I suggest building the crescendo around the synthesis of your speech. Recall that the synthesis is your core message distilled into a single phrase. Recall also that we use public speaking as a platform to provoke action by our audience. The crescendo brings these two together. Let me explain this point with an example.

As mentioned in my biography, I lecture on lecturing, helping to build the capacity of academics who wish to engage their students better. One strategy I adopt—highlighted throughout this book—involves borrowing devices from the spaghetti western genre. I explained this practice in a lecture. The works of Sergio Leone, the true spaghetti western master informed that lecture, but so did John Sturges' The Magnificent Seven (yes, I'm aware it's a brutal remake of Akira Kurosawa's Seven Samurai). Building on the motif, I shared seven devices with the audience: the crescendo was number six. My synthesis was simple enough: being engaging requires not just riveting information but also delivery techniques that stimulate. I linked this to the practice of experimentation, encouraging the audience to draw inspiration from an array of sources when developing their craft.

What crescendo did I opt for? It was my seventh magnificent technique or what I term no happy endings (see the penultimate chapter). To summarise, this phrase means that, irrespective of your effort, commitment, and techniques, you will never satisfy some members of the audience. And I do not mean the Curmudgeons alone. Audiences are naturally heterodox, so we can never be sure how they will respond to our practice. Some audiences members celebrate my lack of slides while others lament this. Some judges appreciate my gregarious style while others wish I were more subdued. Some of my clients appreciate how demanding I am while others would prefer more mollycoddling. You should accept that, no matter what you do, some dissatisfaction is inevitable. If you have not learnt this lesson yet, you will quickly realise that public speaking is a lonely and risky business. If you take on this activity, for gain or for fame, you will experience your fair share of disappointment. My conclusion to the professors was that they should not expect happy endings. Instead, they should better engage their students because they want to be more proficient at their craft and not because they need affirmation from others.

Several of the attendees thought my crescendo was both despairing and dispiriting, and they commandeered much of the Q&A to probe me on this single point. Without claiming to be cleverer than I am, this was my aim. Audiences remember crescendos. I did not want them to dwell on devices two or five. I could have chosen a distinct set of six devices and the talk would have had the same effect. What mattered was the seventh, for the point of the speech was to empower academics to break the mould when teaching (the organiser asked me to encourage this). Academic lecturing is stale because academics recreate what they experienced—what they suffered—during their education. Not only is this dispiriting for audiences, but it is also demoralising for speakers, who get bored themselves, and public speakers are notorious for tiring of their own voices. While some speakers experiment, many are weary of the negative response and thus play it safe by reproducing familiar strategies. In this way, my talk was mostly a call-to-action, and the crescendo reflected this.

Like the controversy, expect the crescendo of your narrative to raise eyebrows and prompt debate. This is to your advantage. It ensures that the audience is engaging with your speech. In music, a crescendo is the loudest point. In public speaking, it is the most memorable one.

*

Should all oral performances resemble a Ted Talk? Of course not. Ted Talks are light-hearted, often superficial, and intended to edu-tain. They often feel like sitcom episodes and I cannot remember any of the sitcoms I watched in my youth. However, while I may not recall the finer points of every speech I attend, I remember most stories I encounter: ones I read, those I've heard, or which I've watched. What happens to Darth Vader in George Lucas' Star Wars series? Too easy.

Stories stay with us as each element combines to trigger an almost Pavlovian response. We will experience hundreds of thousands if not millions of them. So common are stories and storytelling devices that we respond on a subconscious level. By capitalising on this format, you ensure that, at the very least, your audience is paying attention. Whether you captivate them with your story, whether they tell their friends about it will depend on your ability to deploy the skills detailed in this book.

9

MIND MAPS

In the preceding chapter, I described the narrative model of communication—storytelling—and encouraged its liberal application to public speaking. Rarely will you convey your message in a more accessible and engaging manner. A crucial point that I only touched upon is your *representation* of the story to yourself. For a moment, consider how you *think* about and *remember* stories, autobiographies for example. What I wish to draw your attention to is the difference between the way we think about stories and the way we tell them. This provides the premise for this chapter and the premise for the mind map model I encourage you to adopt.

As per the adage, the devil is in the details. I learned this lesson while working as a lawyer: woe betide the advocate who eschews precision as victory or defeat is often a hair's breadth apart. However, the adage has less purchase when applied to storytelling or to 'story thinking'.

Story thinking is a brutal concept, but it captures the essence of this lesson. When we tell stories, details are essential. Details provide personality to the characters and texture to the landscapes. Details provoke and stimulate us as we visualise the story unfolding, sometimes imagining ourselves as protagonists. Some details can be excessive, even superfluous, and distract from the whole.

Recall my example of Tolkien and his Lord of the Rings trilogy. Tom Bombadil is a much loved and much loathed character in the text, so loathed that they have exorcised him from most derivative works. Why? The details Tolkien provides are excruciatingly long and exhausting. 'Get to the point', his detractors say. Tolkien's mistake relates not to his story thinking but to his storytelling. To be more precise, it's not Tolkien's imagination that lets us down but his articulation of the character.

One of the greatest flaws of public speakers is how they perceive their speech. They treat it as a sacred text, committing to its delivery in a predetermined order. While scripted speeches have their place, in most instances, these are best avoided for three reasons. First, reading a speech requires a unique set of skills from those needed to be an effective public speaker. Unfortunately, most speakers equate reading aloud with public speaking and thus fail in their preparation. Second, since most people are even worse public readers than they are public speakers, disengagement is more acute as is the loss of confidence that accompanies it. No one likes contrived, and few things are more contrived than a poorly delivered scripted speech. Third, a scripted speech acts as a barrier between you and the audience. You are in dialogue with your speech just as your speech is in dialogue with your audience. Communication between you and the audience only begins once your speech ends, assuming there is a Q&A.

Instead of treating your speech as a text, think of it as process, an activity, and eventually, a work of art. You cannot script a football match, a painting, or a kiss. You can plan for them and imagine how they will unfold. Perhaps you can anticipate your behaviour but, in all instances, there is no script. The same is true for how we perceive stories and how we should perceive public speaking.

When we think of a story, we do not recite a text to ourselves. Instead, we imagine a mix of elements including protagonists, moods, feelings, or endings. This thought process is more granular than headlines but not as precise as prose. There is a healthy middle point that we settle upon. When urged to articulate the story to someone else, we tell it with greater nuance. However, as is natural, we introduce and censor details according to the context, circumstances, and audience. By reacting to our environment, the story develops, allowing us to connect to the listener, and for them to connect to the story. While the same is true for speeches, few speakers practise this skill.

Anxiety is an obvious reason for this state of affairs. Ask someone to stand up and deliver a speech without preparation. Beyond our megalomaniac friends, most will experience a lightning bolt of dread. By scripting the speech, we placate our anxiety, knowing that we have the text we need. At a minimum, we are certain not to leave anything vital out. I wrote this book, in part, to help people who become anxious in front of audiences. Techniques that make you more effective will also make you more confident, eroding your anxiety though not eliminating it altogether.

There is a less obvious reason: the grudge I have toward scripts. It is common for speakers to prepare a script when deciding what to say. However, once a speaker completes a script, it is difficult, almost impossible for them to deviate. When we formulate ideas in a specific arrangement, the script takes on a life of its own. We come to believe that a break from the script will scupper the whole. Contrast the rigidity of a scripted speech with the flexibility of a planned one. As I made clear in the 'preparation' section, we should plan our speeches. We decide structure, content, illustrations, tone, and message before we stand up. Planning, however, does not mean scripting. We afford ourselves flexibility to adapt to the circumstances as they unfold, but also to build rapport with the audience.

Planned speeches are more challenging than scripted ones. We walk into the room with some doubt, perhaps even worry as we have not committed to a text. It is a skill that you must practice before you achieve the comfort needed to succeed with this model. It's worth emphasizing that planning is not the same as improvising. I have witnessed a handful of people attempt speeches off the cuff and almost all flopped. Without planning, we lack structure assuring that we ramble, itself the death knell of audience interest.

Those who wish to learn to improvise should read my blog posts on this technique. It is fulfilling but, like public reading, demands a distinct set of skills.

Planned performances sit somewhere between script and improvisation. However, they are also miles apart for the cognition needed to conceptualise a performance is far removed from the type needed to draft a text. Enter the mind map.

*

During my years as a lawyer, I prepared three types of materials for court appearances: slides, notes, and lists of keywords. Slides were useful in illustrating the information I presented; my notes played the part of the script; and the keywords highlighted themes of submission. This was overkill. I confused myself, the judge, and the jury with the plethora of materials I relied upon. Information that I omitted from the slides and notes never made it into my submission, irrespective of how either the judge or the jury responded (or how opposing counsel objected). My logic and performance were wonky as I placed myself in a straightjacket that stifled any intellectual creativity.

In quick succession, I abandoned both slides and notes, opting to keep only the keywords. Imagine the scene; it was unlikely to inspire much confidence. Judges witnessed me fumble through my pocket for a scruffy piece of paper—the back of a receipt, for example—on which I scribbled several words in proper lawyer scroll. To add insult to injury, I placed the scrap on the desk in plain sight of my horrified clients. While this approach sounds uninspiring, I should say that my appearances were effective. It was a trial by fire. Court appearances range from a few minutes to a few days, yet all I had were a few words on paper scraps.

Any barrister reading this book will recognise the practice (though perhaps not the scraps of paper). Barristers learn to be flexible as there is no telling when the judge will interrupt. Which they do often. Without mastery over the material and public speaking techniques, the judge's interventions will easily embarrass us. Over time, you either become adept at compressing your submissions into keywords and to expand on demand or you accept being pasted by the judge. When I joined academia, I applied this courtroom strategy to the lecture theatre.

My early days teaching earned me great evaluations from peers and students alike, and many of the lectures are available via YouTube so you can see for yourself. Having clocked hundreds of thousands of views—and I remind you that these are law lectures—I am confident I did something right. I was, however, unimpressed with the lack of professionalism that my materials conveyed. While some would see this as a sign of confidence, I regarded it as sloppy preparation that undermined my credibility. The model was effective, but the articulation was inadequate. I improved it by converting my scraps of paper into mind maps.

*

Mind maps are visual representations of ideas and concepts. We locate connections between information, and arrange them accordingly. Mind maps differ from text in two key ways. First, text is linear: just as the letters move in a prescribed direction, so too does the information follow a trajectory, comprising a beginning, an end, and a progression. In contrast, mind maps represent ideas from a bird's-eye view. They are useful in breaking away from artificial linearity, allowing the author to conceptualise a framework that is more representative of their message.

Second, text is analytical. In this book, for example, I arrange the information in a specific order. While there is creativity to the arrangement, we must distinguish between conceptualising information (an artistic act) from articulating it (an analytical one). In contrast, mind maps balance our brain's ability to engage in both artistic and analytic activities. As we operate from a bird's-eye view, we are more flexible and adaptable with the subject. To illustrate, consider the effort required to alter a page or even a paragraph in a document. The implications are wide reaching, but it is difficult for us to infer what these might be unless we review the entire text while accounting for our amendment. A mind map is more malleable and we can swap concepts at will. At all times, the complete picture is on display allowing us to assess the implications immediately.

In this way, I could add much more texture to the material on my scraps of paper and, obviously, to my lectures. While building a lecture out of a handful of keywords is a useful skill, it leaves much to top levels of mastery and to chance. What happens on a bad day? The scrap of paper will prove insufficient. Improvisation can be memorable but, as I argued before, for the wrong reasons. By keeping a mind map or two at your disposal, you provide yourself with prompts for an in-depth exploration of the topic at hand. As I explained, while the keywords approach is a higher risk, scripted speeches leave you vulnerable to the vagaries of the moment: its linearity makes it near impossible to change on the spot. The mind map provides a happy medium.

I conclude this subsection with mention of the greatest advantage offered by the mind map: flexibility. Not only is a mind map flexible during the conceptualisation phase, but it is also malleable during delivery. Prior to my speech, I scan my map. As a mind map involves the pictorial representation of keywords, a pen is all I need to make a quick change. More valuable is the ability to adapt the map during the actual speech. I often swap sections or alter the order. Those of you interested in seeing this first hand are welcome to request the mind maps I use for my podcasts and listen to them alongside the document. You will notice how I sway between topics, substituting portions of the map or skipping them altogether. I make these decisions on the spot as I adjust to the circumstances, feel, and mood of the room (see Chapter 16).

A mind map provides this level of flexibility, the competent practice of which will make you much more captivating and memorable as a speaker.

*

There is another advantage to mind maps, one that I allude to above. Mind maps are malleable; that much is clear. But what makes them easy to work with? By visualising your ideas and concepts across a map rather than a text, we identify the connections and make the big picture apparent. The speaker enjoys freedom of the map and can choose which sections they wish to stress just as they can soften others.

In this way, and in contrast to scripted speeches, mind maps stimulate greater mastery and confidence. Scripts are like training wheels: just as the safeguard keeps a child's bicycle upright, so too is a speaker supported by their script. However, a safeguard can become a safety blanket. While training wheels make children feel safe, they also hinder their development. It creates a dependence as children come to fear their removal. The same is true for speakers. Despite clocking hundreds of hours of public speaking, the thought of eschewing notes or text-heavy lecture slides can send many speakers into a tailspin. Their notes act like crutches and they fear standing on their own two feet.

Mind maps create no such dependence. Speakers become more confident in their abilities and better at using their skills. Recall my earlier remark: I rely on my mind maps, yes, but they trigger the knowledge I already possess and can deliver. At no point do I engage in a slavish recitation of the material in the mind map. In fact, I could not even if I wanted to. Reciting a visual representation would produce nothing more than gibberish. By avoiding the training wheels, I ensure that every performance is a unique artistic creation that people remember. While captivating audiences, I enhance my speaking abilities too.

The mind map eventually takes the form of an accordion. To understand the metaphor, reflect on the rigidity of the scripted speech once more. A script includes all the information we deem necessary, arranged in a pre-defined format. It is difficult to adapt when things go awry. The rigidity forces us to amputate a section of our speech, creating an incongruity in the structure. Worse, if we are running short on time, the only option available to us is to quicken the pace, losing audience members with each turbo boost. If we overestimate the length of our speech, we must resort to elongating the performance, either by adding impromptu fillers or, as happens frequently, slowing down, an act that can make even the most sober individual look silly.

Mind maps, yet again, are different. Malleability and mastery combine to produce the accordion form. We can compress and expand an accordion on demand. Each act produces a distinct sound and, when combined, generates a bespoke rendition. The same is true for a mind map. Let me explain with an example.

At a symposium in Dublin in 2019, the organisers slotted me alongside a beast of a speaker I have great admiration for. We were each allocated thirty minutes, with another thirty for questions and answers. Chiming in via videoconference, the beast would open and I would close. Five minutes before our start time, he notified the organisers of an emergency that would prevent him from speaking. While some might think this poor form, life takes precedence over professional commitments and his emergency was genuine. The organisers enquired if I could speak for longer (to avoid disrupting the schedule). While I would normally discourage speakers from accepting any last-minute alterations to a speech, I was sympathetic to their predicament. I played up the request, pausing, reflecting, anguishing, before reluctantly agreeing. All of this was for show. More time meant I could develop my speech and further impress the audience. What gave me this confidence? It was the mind map. A mind map allows me to deliver a speech in fifteen or in forty-five minutes. Mind maps allow the speaker to adapt to changing circumstances in a way that a scripted speech makes impossible. Instead of racing along a set route, you veer into the forest, relying on your fitness and navigation skills to lead you out safely.

Adaptability, malleability, and mastery are the key takeaways of the mind map approach, ensuring that your speech flows irrespective of the circumstances you face.

*

I began this chapter with a hideous concept: story thinking. Three thousand words later and it is still a clunker even if its meaning is, I hope, much clearer now. While public speaking can involve storytelling, preparation for and delivery is best thought of through the lens of story thinking. In our minds, we arrange stories as a multiplicity of elements, all of which, despite being jumbled together, are accessible to us in an instant. Such is the nature of stories that we can re-tell them to accommodate changing circumstances. We should treat speeches similarly, facilitating greater flexibility and dynamism in the delivery. Dynamism, to be clear, is essential to being captivating and memorable.

Story thinking is not too far removed from big picture thinking, where we see elements from a bird's-eye view. An eagle can home in on a mouse and swoop down for dinner one moment and swiftly retreat to the skies to scan the horizons the next. You, too, should aim for this high-level ability, adopting techniques that nurture a big picture outlook. Scripted speeches and slides do the opposite, providing a static arrangement of information. Public speaking, however, is not an arrangement of information but a performance that conveys information to an audience. By committing to scripted speeches, speakers stifle themselves. It is the equivalent of mounting a single-speed bicycle with fixed handlebars. Sure, you can pedal faster or slower; you can also lean your weight to redirect your trajectory. Yet, the bike contrives your movements, forcing you to work within parameters that shackle rather than liberate.

I prefer mind maps to scripts for their ability to centre story thinking. With greater malleability and mastery, comes greater fluidity. Speakers who show command over their speech enhance their credibility. This does not mean that you eschew detail: a mind map should be fairly comprehensive, acting as a pictorial of the whole and providing prompts for different pathways. Key elements, phrases, and even gags are suitable for a mind map. It's not important what you include or exclude. Only you know the choices you make. What matters most are the interconnections a mind map stimulates. By breaking the script addiction, your speeches will eventually become as available to you as your stories, allowing you to showcase your abilities with both creativity and credibility.

10

TONE AND VOICE

One of the splendid gifts of biology is the breadth of the human voice. They are much like snowflakes: identical in composition but unique in feel. While this claim may sound eccentric, we feel voices. Consider for a moment a sound or an accent you regard as sensual and juxtapose this alongside the sound of fingernails on a blackboard. Each provokes a unique reaction and a different sentiment.

As per my earlier comments, public speaking is mainly non-verbal, if by non-verbal we mean not word-based. Tone and intonation (more on the difference shortly) matters not because of what we hear but because of what we feel based upon what we hear. Is an entire chapter needed to examine tone? Combined with the next two chapters on movement and tempo, this one on tone will enhance your capabilities as a public speaker.

In the following chapter, I divide my exploration of tone into two parts: substantive and technical tones. The substantive tone is the general character you convey through your speech. Do you opt for an aspirational, combative, exuberant, reflective, or perplexed tone? To answer this question, bring together the topic, audience, and action you wish to engender. Barristers, for example, are notorious for two tones—convivial or pugnacious—neither of which is appropriate in most circumstances, and the insincerity creates a barrier between speaker and audience. Substantive tones will influence your language, both verbal and bodily, your style of dress, and your movement. In my experience, reflection on substantive tone is often superficial: I will give the best darn speech I can! I am here to win! I will have them eating out of the palm of my hands. Proclamations such as these are more distracting than helpful, articulating a trivial aspiration instead of a suitable tone.

Technical tone is the second variety, which I discuss later in this chapter. I refer to it as intonation or dynamics, as it's described in music theory. Intonation is the rise and fall of our voice. Think pitch. Musicians engage with intonation at a far deeper level. Dynamics represent the varying levels of sound that appear in a musical performance. For example, a musical arrangement may begin in hushed tones before spiralling upwards into a booming canon (a crescendo) before shifting into elongated or staccato sounds. While a consistent beat may undergird the whole—think metronome—any musical arrangement worth its salt will transition dynamically, not only across instruments and vocals but also across sound itself. Cadence is only tangentially relevant to dynamics, and I treat this in Chapter 13 under the heading tempo.

With a firm grasp of substantive tones and dynamics, your speeches will gain greater character and texture as your voice becomes an instrument in its own right, deployed to serenade your audience on cue.

SUBSTANTIVE TONE

Since audience, occasion, and subject vary, so too must your tone adapt to the surroundings. To recall an earlier lesson, just as an argument has no nature referent, neither does a speech possess a natural tone. One of the most important reasons tone varies relates to your appeal. Typecast actors see their potential diminish. Directors call upon them to fill certain roles only. The same is true for speakers who operate with a single tone.

For illustrative purposes, let me recollect an old barrister I knew in Los Angeles. In legal practice, California is the litigation capital of the world where many trial lawyers, of varying quality, make (and lose) their fortunes. Los Angeles courts are especially susceptible to displays of thespian overreach.

In a dispute between my client, a multinational corporation, and the clients of the old barrister, a pensioner couple, his clients had the upper hand. As my client was in the wrong, our aim was damage limitation and negotiating a settlement. As a seasoned trial lawyer, he knew the drill; so did I and the judge. While I was angling for a rapid settlement, he was playacting for his clients and for the judge. During one court appearance (to discuss a minor scheduling matter), he proclaimed that my client's behaviour was such a travesty of human decency that, at a minimum, rabid dogs should set loose on them. The behaviour was egregious, and the imagery repulsed the judge.

In court and in chambers, this barrister practised one tone: to the death. Even where he had the advantage, he lacked the oratory nous to leverage the sympathy of the court. Instead, the ad hominem attacks against my client and, as I still recall, against me, caused us to change strategies. While he was busy with theatrics, my team and I were cajoling the judge and jury at every opportunity. As the judge became more irate with the barrister, they became more sympathetic towards us, resulting in the close calls going our way and shifting momentum in our favour. Jury members rolled their eyes or laughed in exasperation at every objection. He hit peak buffoonery when he yelled at the judge. [To dispel any doubt, you should never raise your voice to a judge.] As expected, he eventually won the case. However, his poisoning of the waters meant that the jury awarded compensation far lower than what we would have settled for.

It is easy for me to cherry-pick my examples and to speculate about how a jury might have acted had the tone been different. I stand by this example, nevertheless. Expert orators appreciate the power of tone and deploy different ones during their performance. The very best orators can swap tones midway through a speech, stressing the point they are making. Amateurs adopt a single style, which they then practise excessively (often exclusively). Not only do they inhibit their own development, but they also undermine the effectiveness of their performances: if your tone is always combative, everyone will look like an enemy, even potential allies. Likewise, if your tone is always playful, you will inspire neither credibility nor confidence. Tone is a tool that smooths your connection to the audience, enhancing your appeal along the way.

Next, you must adapt your tone to the occasion and circumstances. When speaking about this, I often reference an interview I held with the University of Hong Kong. As I often do in speeches, I peppered my performance with a few jokes. Members of the hiring committee were unimpressed with my jovial tone, preferring their academics to exude sober gravitas. Contrary to what I intended, I came across as flippant. My interview was over before it began.

Selecting the tone thus requires reflection on the audience and the action you wish to elicit. Your aim is to develop two capacities: to identify a suitable tone and to articulate your speech in it. Identifying the correct tone is easier than it appears. My first act is to imagine myself as an audience member: what do I expect? Returning to the belligerent barrister, I assure you that the jury did not expect him to pick fights. While there is value in challenging your audience, these tactics are best used sporadically to break the monotony rather than as a consistent mode of delivery. People find confrontation exhausting. Other tones have greater purchase across a range of circumstances and topics: argumentative (rather than combative), exploratory, motivational, and reflective tones, for example. An argumentative approach is appropriate if you are challenging accepted wisdom in the same way that an inquisitive tone would be suitable when pondering alternative avenues.

Despite the many tones available, only a couple will suit your speech. I proceed via a process of elimination, removing unsuitable tones. With those remaining, I assess my aspirations and capacities. For example, while I am adept at humour, I am terrible with light-hearted speeches. My speeches tend towards the meditative and provocative. It is not uncommon for audiences to breathe a collective sigh of relief when I conclude. So, even if I decide that a humorous tone is desirable, I am unlikely to opt for it due to my personal limitations. Tone can open as many doors as it can close and you should reflect on the tone suitable to the occasion.

DYNAMICS

I reiterate my opening statement: voices are consistent in character but unique in feel. I have never encountered two people with the same voice; even identical twins sound different. While I may envy Andre 3000, Idris Elba, and Joe Rogan for their deep baritones, for good or for bad, there is little we can do about our voices. They are not as malleable as our accents. The point may be obvious but it does not make it any less important, for most public speakers lament their voices, wishing they sounded different. While we cannot sound like someone else, we can manipulate the dynamics of our voices to make ourselves more captivating.

To understand dynamics, reflect on speakers who do not use them. Though the content might interest, steady is dull, and I am not the only one to have fallen asleep when listening to a monotonous speaker. It is no surprise that hypnotists favour this intonation just as it is equally understandable why illusionists would avoid it. To be clear, monotony does not come from being bland, indifferent or soft-spoken, though these qualities are unlikely to help your cause. Monotony is the product of steady and predictable speech patterns. We still hear them, but we are no longer listening.

What are dynamics? I want you to think of volume, tempo, and range. They are the features of our voices that can stimulate engagement. Opera singers, for example, practice dynamics just as much as they practice singing: how high, low, wide, or narrow can they make their voices? What effect will a sharp staccato (pronouncing each word sharply detached from one another) have in contrast to a lengthy legato (talking in a smooth flowing manner without breaks between words)? Dynamics bring your voice—and thus your speech—alive.

I begin with volume as it is one of the easiest to manipulate. Your aim is to lower and raise the decibel level in line with the importance of the point you are making. Both whispers and bellows are suitable for key points because they focus the mind and thus your audience's attention. We use the mid-range for everything else. Do not misunderstand me: avoid speaking in the mid-range for more than a short while lest you fall into the steady and predictable trap. Spikes or drops in volume help stress key points and words with each transition, disrupting the lull in your intonation and reawakening your audience's attention.

Tempo or pace is also at your disposal. Musicians calculate the speed of the underlying beat, aligning the tempo with the music they produce. For example, ballads are meditative and demand a lento (or slow tempo) while dance songs are lively and thus more suited to an allegro (or fast tempo). Speakers overlook tempo. Rather than slowing or speeding up according to the talk, they focus on the length of the performance. Yet, speeches are as intertwined with speed as is music. Two exercises that I require of my students is, first, to calculate their tempo and, second, to practice alternating it. The first is the easier of the two: record yourself speaking at your normal pace for 30 seconds. Following this, re-record yourself speaking at a preferred pace. When listening back to both, tally the words and determine whether you are naturally more lento or allegro. For the second exercise, you should speed up and slow down your tempo during your speech. Just as changes in volume disrupt the monotony, so do changes in tempo prevent your audience from becoming too comfortable or distracted.

I left range (pitch) for last as it is a hard skill to master. We often assess the quality of a singer according to their vocal range. Without formal musical training, it is difficult to manipulate your range or to reproduce a precise pitch on demand. It is near impossible for me, for example, to know whether I have hit a G or an F as I cannot distinguish them. You need not worry about this either. As I play with volume and tempo, I also play with pitch to highlight specific points, though I do this less frequently than with the other two. I mention it because it is useful for those who master their voices and wish to add another dynamic to the mix.

*

Hearing is a vital sense, providing an endless stream of information to the listener. Yet, most sounds are background noise and affect us indirectly, much like volume, tempo and range affect our experience of a speech. To illustrate the point, at present I am writing this chapter while sitting in a flat in Barcelona. At least five or six sounds are discernible: a loud hum emanating from the refrigerator; the occasional muffled voices of passersby; the clicking of my laptop keys; car horns galore; and the music booming from my speakers (Stevie Wonder, if you were wondering). Each sound affects my concentration. I rarely play music with lyrics when writing, but I am doing so to override the sounds of the refrigerator and tourists. Despite my best efforts, I remain distracted, each impeding my focus and muddying my prose. Along with being a conduit for information, sound is also a stimulant. Throughout this chapter, I explain how you can leverage tone to your advantage while cautioning against its nefarious underbelly.

I urge you not to overlook this point. My statement about hearing as a vital sense comes with a qualification: during oral performances, hearing is the most important sense of all. Irrespective of how pleasing you are, audiences will lose interest in your appearance within a few minutes. They may revert to you or your slides now and again, but they will return to your voice, which is what you want. Neglecting intonation equates to an athlete disregarding their diet. While diet may not determine whether Messi scores a goal, it will affect his fitness levels and performance, and the spectators' enjoyment.

The same is true for public speakers. I encourage you to reflect on intonation at two levels: first, the character of the tone needed—

which tone is suitable for your speech—and, second, the dynamics that will stimulate the audience's engagement. Mastering these skills takes time, but the gains will help you distinguish between being capable and being mesmerising.

11

TEMPO AND RHYTHM

I am an early riser. My best hours are between 0500 and 1600, maybe 1630. Throughout my career as a barrister, I arrived at the office by 0615 and departed by 1600. My schedule irked colleagues because I had completed a half-day's work before they set foot in the office. Morning court submissions, just like morning trials, were my bread and butter. The judge and jury may still have been nibbling on theirs, but I was barrelling down the fast lane with my clients in tow. My schedule as an academic has remained much the same as I am at my laptop by 0600. I would gladly lecture this early if my university allowed it. In fact, at the University of Auckland, I volunteered for the 0800 slot, three days a week. These remain some of my best lectures, and the 300-plus student enrolment suggests others concurred.

What does my circadian rhythm have to do with public speaking? Some may have already guessed it. I learned early on that my rhythm is incongruous to that of others. While I wake up with all cylinders firing, others prefer a tranquil morning, creating a gap between me and my audience. If I was jamming to Outkast on my stroll to the office, my audience was only just awakening to a ballad, maybe even a requiem. Such was my experience with colleagues, judges, and students, who preferred a later start time. Since I could not change my rhythm, I needed a strategy for mediating the incongruity. Tempo provided the answer.

Borrowing from music theory, tempo is the pace of a piece of music. To better understand how disruptive an incongruity in tempo can be, imagine a ballerina pirouetting to Metallica or a couple Lindy Hopping to Mozart. What makes these pairings awkward is the pace or tempo that each operates at. With incongruous pairings, it is not an issue of moving too slowly or too fast but of the parties moving at different tempos. With music and dance, this translates into an incongruent logic, as it does for speakers and audiences. When tempo is out of sync, the speaker and audience are on alternate wavelengths. Neither slowing down nor speeding up will make a difference.

In this chapter, I explain this point by dividing the topic into two parts. In the first, I speak to cognitive processing, for this is where the disconnect manifests. In the second, I explain how you should practise tempo to deliver speeches at a pace suitable to your audiences.

COGNITIVE PROCESSING

Cognition is the scientific term for thought. What does it mean to think? Thought happens when we apply our minds to something. Applying one's mind is a complex activity involving multiple operations, which is why we distinguish between types and acts of cognition. Cognitive processing is the term for clusters of cognition.

The notion of clusters is a useful starting point when contemplating cognition. We must think to walk, kick a ball, type on a laptop, identify familiar and unfamiliar scents, fumble over a new electronic device, and to speak and listen. Walking and kicking balls are motor acts, just as listening is a sensory act. While these do not appear to involve any thinking, each requires that we gather and apply information gained from the environment before us. That is cognition. To ride a bicycle, we must pedal, balance, navigate, observe, and react. We can act intelligently when riding a bicycle, just as we can do so in the world based when we can process information efficiently. Before I move on to cognitive processes relevant to public speaking, I will draw on a football example.

Football aficionados regard Pep Guardiola as one of the greatest football managers of the current era. Having reviewed some of his manuals—available online—I can vouch for the understanding and vision he possesses. Few people have transformed football into science as shrewdly as he has, including developing a training technique that exemplifies the centrality of cognitive processes to success in modern football. Twenty two players are positioned throughout the pitch with the coach lurking in the centre. Once he blows the whistle, the game begins. There is a catch, however: there is no ball. While this sounds ludicrous, upon reflection, there is genius in his technique. Modern footballers possess such athleticism that they can move from one end of the pitch to the other in mere seconds. Following the ball, while still essential, is no longer the linchpin of victory. What matters is your position in relation to the ball and to the other players. An ability to read the game and to predict the moves of teammates and opponents alike determines the outcome. Much like chess, football is a game of strategy that involves the proficient cognition, hence the genius behind the technique: it compels the players to think before they act and to speed up their anticipation of the game.

In cognitive sciences, researchers distinguish between two types of processes: basic and complex. Each category is relevant for excelling at public speaking. Basic processes include sensation and perception and are, mostly, practiced unconsciously. When walking down a crowded street, we perceive the movements of others and shift our position accordingly. More relevant to public speaking are two other basic processes: attention and memory. Memory is self-explanatory so I will say little about it (though I encourage those who would like to know more about the relationship between memory and public speaking to read my blog post on memory temples). However, for this chapter and to be successful at public speaking, understanding the implications of attention is vital.

Stimuli affect us every moment of the day, demanding that we learn to distinguish between stimuli of interest, importance, and irrelevance. How do we do this? We have learned to practice varied levels of attention: alternative, divided, fleeting, focused, selective, and sustained. Imagine yourself driving along the motorway, through a section undergoing public works, while sipping a coffee, listening to your companion speaking on their phone, and with music in the background. What exactly are you paying attention to? The answer 'everything' is inaccurate. You are aware of everything, but your levels of attention vary. If they didn't, you would not survive the drive. Toward the road, you focus your attention; to your friend's conversation, to your coffee, and to the music your attention is selective if not fleeting. We always divide our attention, choosing what we need to prioritise. When we can no longer focus on essential stimuli and silence irrelevant ones, they become interferences that hinder our ability to think. Recall when you asked a child to keep the noise down while you concentrate on something else.

For today's listeners, the task is doubly difficult. Besides the inherent challenges identified in Chapter 7, we must account for the proliferation of technology use and the impact this has on the attention of audiences. Observe the person sitting across from you at a cafe or on a bus and count the number of times they switch applications on their smartphone. The speed and frequency at which people transition from one activity to another is breath-taking. Two aspects of this practice are most troubling for public speakers. First, listeners presume that they apply their attention fairly, irrespective of the number of transitions they practice. People cannot appreciate that divided attention dilutes their engagement with any single activity. Second, the use of technology is addictive. It is difficult for the user to stop using their technology even when they want to. Public speakers must therefore adapt to an increasingly crowded environment.

You may have noticed that I have yet to say anything about complex cognitive processes. To practice complex cognition, we require a blend of abilities. These include multiple intelligences, varying forms of thinking, and the application of language. While we can practice basic cognitive processes with minor effort—e.g. memorise the following number: 78789696—complex cognitive processes require attention and time, such as identifying the pattern embedded in the number you just memorised. Meta-cognitive thinking or the ability to settle on strategies for navigating complex problems is, possibly, the most important complex process of all. I say more about this in my concluding chapter.

What does this mean for public speakers? If you cannot persuade your audience to pay attention, you will fail at prompting the higher levels of engagement needed for them to become captivated by your talk. Not only will they need the football to practice the game, but they will also think you are mad for proposing otherwise. Without capturing attention, complex cognitive processes are impossible.

Happily, there is a technique for this: manipulating tempo.

THE POWER OF PACE

Pace (tempo) is vital to success in life. Pick a pace that is too quick and you will burn out. Choose a tempo that is too slow and you are likely to get bored or, worse, to see others run laps around you. Chefs and cyclists know the importance of tempo well and are the best pace setters I know. The former must ensure that mains are ready to go shortly after patrons finish their entrees and that dessert, prepared much earlier in the day, appears as fresh as if it just came out of the oven. They have to replicate this across dozens of tables, with patrons who begin at varied times and eat at different speeds, all while mediating the complaints and snafus that invariably disrupt whatever plan they began with. Similarly, competitive cyclists cover interminable distances at incredible speeds, in collaboration with teammates and in competition with others, across several weeks, on diverse terrain, and with varying climatic conditions. They do all this while managing their caloric intake, hydration, and fatigue (not to mention their sanity), and maintaining a consistent pace for hundreds, if not thousands of kilometres. Tempo is key and if either sous-chefs or support riders are out of sync with the pacesetter, chaos ensues. Much effort thus goes into ensuring that the tempo is manageable for all parties, a skill public speakers should develop.

At the first level, a speaker must be mindful of the tempo of their talk. Is it pitched at the right level and does it progress at the right pace? The quality of a restaurant or the strength of a team depends on its members. Leaders are aware of this and adjust according to patterns and tendencies the members exhibit. When are they most alert; which dish is the least complicated; which mountain requires a greater caloric boost? The same is true for speakers: how will you account for food coma when your speech begins just after lunch; do you speed up or slow down if you notice the audience drifting; will props improve or hinder the explanation of an especially tough point?

At the second level, a speaker must be mindful of the audience and their capacity to keep up with the speech. Again, chefs and pacesetters account as much for their strengths and weaknesses as they do for those of their teammates. Speakers are notorious for focusing on themselves and their speech while assuming that others will keep up. I have even witnessed speakers feel offended when the audience's attention wanes. Yet, it is too facile to scapegoat the audience for their loss of concentration. A proficient speaker can do much to help the audience keep pace. Three considerations are especially useful here.

GET THEM ON THE SAME PAGE

Never underestimate the importance of beginnings. Too often, speakers begin with the classic 'Hello, my name is...'. Others opt to thank an endless list of people. Either of these openings cues the audience to continue their conversation, to finish texting, or to daydream a little longer. Your talk hasn't begun. Worse than this is laying out your plan of action or highlighting the key message in the opening minutes. Many audiences will miss this information, forcing you to reiterate it later to the irritation of those who were paying attention.

Instead, treat the beginning as a warm-up: its purpose is to prepare you and everyone for the event to come. Open with a question, a story, or even a prop that shakes your audience out of its natural stupor. With students, I often ask a question that relates to the topic and then offer three answers, comparing one to the next. With judges, I open with an anecdote about myself, or about my client, before segueing into the case. With the public, I tell an eventful story about what brought me there. Each of these warms up the audience. By the time the performance gets underway, I have already secured (most of) the audience's attention.

THE LOOP-BACK

I taught my daughter to ride a bicycle in urban areas. As important as it was for her to learn balance, more important was learning to share the road with cars and manifestations of road rage. She stayed close behind me until I sped up into an intersection, where I slowed down before waving her through. She would continue apace while I caught up to her, checked in, and then moved in front yet again or what I term the loop-back. Cyclists will recognise this practice. To protect a weaker rider, a stronger rider does more. Here, I cleared the route of dangers without disrupting my daughter's tempo.

I practice the loop-back when I speak to ensure that my audience is on track. In any speech, even when interacting with fellow experts, you are at an advantage: you know your talk better than anyone, meaning you are always the stronger rider. It is your duty to loop-back and check in. The loop-back is an effective way of keeping their attention—they must keep up—while also keeping them on track. The benefits are therefore mutual: while the audience catches their breath, you gain valuable information about their attentiveness and capacities.

STRUCTURE AND RECAP

When sous-chefs join a new kitchen, one of their first acts is to check the menu (in fact many of them do this before applying for the job). Why? To understand what chefs expect of them and how their skills are best allocated. Support cyclists are no different. They review the course map and the cycling schedule. If available, they will also consult the team's strategy. Audiences do not have these luxuries. They decide which talks to attend based upon a biography and a blurb (at least when attendance is not mandatory). They can access little information about the speaker and even less about the content. Tempo and tone are absent altogether. Most audiences rely on faith and optimism when choosing which lecture to attend. They count on the speaker to bring them up to speed and to keep them on track. Structures and recaps are invaluable in this regard and in preserving the preferred tempo.

I have already spoken about structure (Chapter 6). What I wish to highlight here is the importance of linking structure to tempo. Just as descending a hill is easier than climbing one, concentrating when rested is less taxing than when tired. What this means is that some moments are more opportune for the delivery of certain types of information than others. To take an easy example, displaying text-heavy slides to your audience during the latter stages of your talk will feel like a sledgehammer to the chest.

When structuring your speech, account for your audience's state of mind. A simple rule is to front-end tough material—when their minds are fresh—and to back-end lessons that you can deliver in light-hearted fashion. I also suggest sprinkling recaps into the structure: these act as spot checks for your audience, helping them mediate their attention themselves. To use our cyclist example once more, a pacesetter does not hide the route map from the support riders. That would be both silly and counterproductive. The pacesetter must trust that their teammates can manage themselves. Access to the map will allow them to plan their hydration, snacks, and rest. In short, the more structured you are, the easier it will be for your audience to keep up with your tempo and to remain attentive to your performance.

*

I opened this chapter by describing the natural incongruity between my circadian rhythm and that of my audiences. Far from undermining my success as a public speaker, this incongruity helped me develop a crucial tool for my repertoire. To secure the audience's attention throughout my speech, I account for both cognitive processing and tempo, two elements that I treat as symbiotic. By considering the type of cognitive processing I expect of audiences, I can identify a suitable tempo. Basic and complex cognitive processes differ in operation and complexity, meaning that I must adjust my pace according to the expected processing time. Once I select a suitable tempo, I use three measures to keep my audience up to speed. I begin by easing them into the topic with a warm-up activity. Next, I loop-back, ensuring that no one falls behind or off the bike altogether. Last, I link the structure of my speech to my tempo, accounting for the audience's rhythm when delivering the information.

Tempo is a handy tool for developing reciprocity with your audience. Despite being a complex skill, it is one of the easiest ways of transforming a monologue into a dialogue and thus involving your audience in your speech. Speakers who see their audiences as participants or even as teammates in their performance are more successful at stimulating complex cognitive processes. By definition, complex processes are more captivating, memorable, and satisfying for all involved.

12

MOVEMENT AND PHYSICALITY

Ninety percent of communication is non verbal. I mention this phenomenon often, both in text and in person. It features a fundamental point about public speaking that speakers often overlook: what you say only weighs lightly on the audience's experience. The gallery is listening, yes, but more significant than this is their sense of your presentation. Your talent for arousing your audience's senses and to spark their thinking will affect how captivating and memorable you are.

Consider a simple example: audiobooks are becoming more popular. Our addiction to devices is the prime culprit, but the ease of recording helps as well. Audiobooks, however, offer a unique experience. When reading books, we imagine the picture the author paints; we conceive the voices of the characters; and sometimes we even fall in love (or hate) with some of these same characters. Our scale of commitment to the book influences our experience much as our mood at the moment does as well. I also listen to audiobooks, though with far less enthusiasm. My experience is distinct, and depends on the quality of the performer and performance: the voice of the author, the intonations they adopt, and the accents they represent. Here, it is the speaker's commitment and mood that produce the experience. Why is this?

Enter a second essential statistic: we forget 90% of what we hear within one hour of hearing it. It is the experience or our memory of the experience that stays with us. Even though audiobooks rely on verbal communication, the experience of the listener depends on non-verbal prompts that we take notice of. Is the speaker animated, irate, or monotonous? Our voice conveys much more than words, and our features make us distinctive.

Public speakers are at thus a disadvantage compared to music bands. Music aficionados do not gauge a band's quality according to the things they say but the experience they deliver. With public speakers, words are central but not as all-encompassing as we presume. You should not fret over this; in fact, it will prove liberating as you cease worrying about every minor word. It will also prove empowering as you realise you have other tools at your disposal. Enter movement.

*

In Chapter 5, I provided a few remarks about movement. My focus was on distinguishing between purposive and habitual hand gestures. The point was simple: gestures should be deliberate and we must endeavour to control whichever ticks we possess. In particular, I emphasised eliminating erratic gesturing: movements that are too fast, too big, or too jerky. Because of their velocity, these tire the audience and are off-putting, even for interested listeners. Instead, practice movements that are slower and smaller. Some coaches prefer speakers to be natural, urging intuitive or mindful public speaking. I think this approach is misguided as I explain throughout the book. We must identify which habits distract and smooth them out through practice. Move, yes, but move calmly and maturely.

Beyond eliminating the noxious, how do we practice movement in a manner that complements our speech? Three concepts are useful to achieving positive movement: animation, stimulation, and association. First, we use our bodies to animate our speech. Second, we move through the room and stimulate interaction with the audience. Third, we create associations between keywords or ideas and specific movements. Some cynics dismiss these as party tricks. They could not be more wrong. Returning to our two statistics, nonverbal communication is the core of an audience's experience; verbal is peripheral. Rejecting positive movement equates to a poker pro playing every hand honestly. They do little more than weaken their position.

I dedicate the rest of the chapter to explaining how you can leverage movement to your advantage. Like the other techniques detailed in this book, practice is key. I encourage you to trial movements in the comfort of your home and to record yourself while doing so. Upon viewing, it will be clear whether your movements subvert or support your performance.

*

First, let's look at animating speech with movement. Quality speakers use their bodies to enhance their speech. This applies to pacing and gestures alike, movements which the speaker should practice. Gestures are part of the performance and, as such, should facilitate the delivery of your message. Obvious gestures include up and down, left and right, big and small. A very simple movement can easily animate each word and idea. Animation has a double effect: clarifying the point and engaging the audience. While these sounds childish, recall what I said earlier: audiences face the unenviable task of remaining attentive from beginning to end. By animating parts of your performance, you assist your audience. They will thank you for your efforts with deeper levels of engagement.

We can take this same point further by applying it to more complex words and ideas: fast and slow, attacking and defending, fear and anger. You can animate each word, idea, sentiment, expression, or act with a gesture. I have sprinted across the stage to signify speed, just as I have mimed running from an attacker. Not only do these actions bolster your message but, when done right, they also add a levity to the performance. You might feel silly, however, when delivered sincerely, each gesture will make you more endearing to the audience. Context is everything, and a lecture theatre is more suitable than a courtroom when miming a football kick. However, four fingers to animate four hundred, an outstretched arm for length, and raised arms to denote fear are appropriate in any setting. Your imagination is your best resource.

*

These last examples tread closely to the second aim of positive movement: to stimulate your audience. Here, I want you to think of emotion and provocation. Just as we deploy words to stimulate, so too can movement help. One of my favourite moves when I feel the audience drifting is to walk into no-go territory. In a courtroom, this involves walking backwards, past the swinging gate, and into the public seating area. Most attendees raise an eyebrow which is the purpose: to snap them out of their stupor. I have done the same in amphitheatres by walking up and down steps, breaking the invisible barrier between speaker and audience. It feels uncomfortable for everyone: the front rows must crane their necks; the back rows must put their mobile phones away; even I must be careful not to stumble along the steps. You stimulate attendees by moving in unpredictable ways.

Many actions are available to stimulate your audience, and almost all of them involve crossing the speaker-audience barrier or being playful. Another personal favourite is to approach an attendee and, mid-sentence, interrupt myself and ask if I may use their water bottle, mobile phone, or even notebook (I never ask for an item they are using). I then display the item as a prop to explain my point. This may involve showing it to the audience, handing it to another student, or even placing it in my pocket. Regardless, the act will surprise most and pull them in as they wait with anticipation for the impromptu act to reach its climax. Again, your imagination is the only limit: you can pretend to break it, throw it, or even devour it. In all instances, reflect on your speech and how this act will complement it.

To provide a few more examples, I have jumped over an imaginary line (to highlight a binary point), danced a jig (to illustrate the many responses we can give to a police officer who asks us for ID without probable cause), and slammed a desk (to feign violence). I delivered each act to draw attention to a vital point in the speech while also inciting an emotional response from the attendees. Push the boundaries when provoking your audience so long as you account for the elements identified above: speed, scope, and frequency.

A caveat is in order before I conclude this section. I carry out each gesture, movement, or act upon myself. I do not involve others, save for when I request someone's object. Even when punching the desk, I punch either my own or one that is unoccupied. Your aim is to provoke your audience, yes, but some of these moves can make people uncomfortable, which is why you keep your hands to yourself. This is an essential point.

In the past, when making a point about physical contact, I asked a male student if I could place my hand on their shoulder and then used this as a lesson about battery and the range of permissible touching. While my choice of a male student was deliberate, and I secured permission before placing my hand on them, it occurred to me afterwards that even this had crossed a line of propriety. I fear neither lawsuits nor censure (though this is a genuine concern for individuals who are delivering lessons to staff and could sexually harass one of them, inadvertently or maliciously). You should practice using your body to stimulate an audience and avoid putting any of your audience members on the spot. I now hover my hand over someone's shoulder when delivering a lesson about battery and permissible touching. I even learned that the effect is more powerful as everyone wonders whether I will touch the individual in question, achieving a higher level of stimulation than if I had just placed my hand on them. Finally, take these observations with a grain of salt: buskers, hypnotists, and illusionists use audience members all the time. My comments apply to formal settings, especially if you find yourself in a workplace or at an institutional event where levels of propriety are more stringent than in street performances or theatre events.

*

The third element is association: think of mnemonics. A mnemonic is a tool deployed to help remember numbers, facts, or a sizeable amount of information and takes the form of a phrase, rhyme, acronym, or even image. For example, in legal theory, I encourage students to think of a parliamentarian in a boxing match with a member of the clergy when learning about the duality between natural law and legal positivism. I then inscribe keywords on their boxing gloves, with each representing a pillar or argument used to bolster their position. Is it a stalemate or does one argument deliver the knockout blow? As you can see, by associating legal theory with a boxing match, the arguments are easier to visualise and remember.

As with animation and simulation, there are no limits when associating words or ideas for your audience. There are, however, two guidelines that I suggest accounting for. First, ensure that the image, acronym or phrase is memorable. Had I associated legal theory with two book titles—Hart's Concept of Law versus Aquinas' Treatise of Law, for example—the students would remember nothing.

Second, you must repeat the association, drilling it into your audience. Even a memorable boxing metaphor requires repetition if the link is to stick. I chose boxing, as it lends itself to a mixture of gestures and images: boxing poses (raising my arms), Hart's name (he shows a lot of 'heart in the ring), or phrases ('on the ropes' and 'knockout punch'). Each time we return to the topic, I tweak the image while drawing the same link to boxing, ensuring that the students associate the dreary world of legal theory with a ring full of prize-fighters.

By capitalising on your audience's associative predispositions—all of us think relationally—you add a useful tool to your kit. Repeated associations are a simple way of enlivening your performance while facilitating complex cognitive processes and thus deeper engagement.

*

I conclude this chapter with some remarks on props. As with other tactics, it is essential that you think about the rationale behind your preferred prop. If it helps your audience recall information or understand a point, or if it lightens the mood, it has value. Some years ago, I attended an event at the Japanese Consulate in London. During the keynote speech, the diplomat drew a mock piece of sushi from her pocket when making a point about the centrality of fish in Japanese cuisine. Despite the time that has passed, I remember her, the movement, and the words: 'oh look, a piece of sushi is in my pocket'. I don't recall the other presenters or remember anything about the event. She, however, is as vivid as the sea.

Props can be invaluable, as it was for the plastic sushi. Choose them carefully and keep it simple, especially if you intend them for associative purposes. Remember, if mnemonics is the aim, it must be available when discussing the same issue. The props you choose and the movements you make will tell the audience much about you. Few expected a timid and sober Japanese diplomat to pull a piece of sushi from her pocket, telling us that there is much more than meets the eye. Even the way we move conveys a lot about our personality. I allude to this throughout this book, sharing elements of your personality will always make a speech more captivating and memorable. Whether you use model cars as props, boxing bouts as metaphors, or Michael Jackson songs as themes, the audience will feel they know you a little better.

PART 3: ADVANCED SKILLS

INTRODUCTION

It should be clear by now that effective public speaking is less a matter of art than it is of technique. Art helps, to be sure, and can distinguish one top speaker from another. More important are the solid foundations upon which we should build a performance. Without adequate preparation, for example, no amount of technique or humour will salvage your speech. No matter how articulate you are, without structure, your audience will quickly disengage, just as they will if you proceed at too swift a pace. By integrating the techniques provided in the preparation and basic skills sections, you will possess a set of methods which will enable you to succeed in public speaking.

However, these skills will be for naught if you do not practice them systematically. All techniques detailed in this book will help you improve. However, just as the book breaks down public speaking into components, you should stagger your study accordingly. Expecting to do everything in your first go is similar to assigning Harry Potter to a child when introducing them to chapter books: too much, too fast will overwhelm and bodes ill for your development. As you practise certain techniques—predictable plot progression, for example—you should only introduce fresh ones such as tempo and tone in due course. Does this mean that you can shelve some skills, at least in the interim? Sort of.

The previous chapters provide sufficient material to get you started and the basis for you to thrive as a public speaker. Much of what I detailed would form the basis of an introductory workshop, and I guide speakers through these elements in coaching sessions. It is a lot like teaching arithmetic or grammar: you must become fluent in the foundations before progressing. However, I also favour exposure to advanced skills early on. A child may be incapable of reading Harry Potter on their own, but they can still learn a fair amount by having it read to them. The same is true of public speaking. You will learn much from watching skilled orators, but only if you understand what they are doing. As you will learn, they build on foundational skills while throwing a few additional techniques into the mix.

In the following chapters, I detail a range of advanced skills. While we still use the basics—self, space, and speech—I introduce more about audience and structure. The initial chapter will help you hone your ability to read the audience. It is no longer a matter of making eye contact or smiling, though these acts remain essential, but also of picking up on cues and responding. Next is a chapter on character development. While characters sound relevant to the narrative that underpins your speech, its breadth is far wider to how you represent yourself and integrate the audience. Using the audience to create a more inclusive climate will also produce a more engaging one. Following this, I provide a chapter on framing and signalling, where I explain how to lead your audience, a little like a sheep dog leads a flock. We frame the speech within boundaries and nudge the audience along with signals. Each of these techniques will allow you to cover a wide range of material while still delivering a focused performance.

Following on from my earlier remarks, do not treat advanced skills as distinct from basic ones. They are more complex, but they are also a natural progression. Reading your audience will help you develop a deeper rapport. It will also allow you to adapt your performance to the room and, as you will quickly learn, no two rooms are identical. What I hope you will come to appreciate about public speaking is that, with the right tools, it can be both a creative and enthralling process. Today, I think of my performances as puzzles: what picture will it yield and how efficient will the process be? My aim with the advanced skills detailed in the coming chapters is to help you see that successful public speaking is not about overcoming your fear, as we hear ad nauseam. To reiterate the point in the preface, you are not afraid because public speaking is frightening but because doing something unfamiliar in front of others is intimidating. By developing both basic and advanced skills, you will understand how to carry out the tasks systematically. You will not have to overcome your fear. With techniques in hand, fear abates.

13

USING THE AUDIENCE TO YOUR ADVANTAGE

The audience is not your enemy. You should etch this phrase at the top of every mind map until it sinks in. Many speakers treat their audiences with either trepidation or suspicion, sometimes both. The initial sentiment is the product of our anxiety: we fear the audience's response. The second results from disappointment: we lament the ambivalence of past audiences. Unfortunately for us, both emotions manifest in neon lights. Audiences pick up on your insecurity and disengage further, provoking a downward spiral in your relationship. Regardless of the sincerity of your feelings, you and your audience will suffer if you approach them with either of these sentiments. Remind yourself that the audience could be elsewhere. Even in situations with compulsory attendance—courtroom, lecture theatre, or boardroom—the audience still turns up. Time is scarce for everyone. While you might feel jittery or disheartened, concede that the audience would not show up were they not curious about what you had to say. Your duty is to reciprocate: first, by respecting them and, second, by delivering a quality performance.

While the audience is not your enemy, neither is it your friend. Audiences come with expectations. They might be there for education, entertainment, information, or boredom. What they are not there for is friendship, even if some audience members try to be-friend you afterwards. Friends spend time with us for many reasons but, unlike with audiences, we have the advantage of their com-mitment and familiarity. Most of our friends will put up with our unpleasant days; audiences will not. If you do not meet their expec-tations, their perception of you will diminish. They will judge your performance and share their judgments with others.

If the audience is neither your enemy nor your friend, then what are they? Simple: the audience. Reflect on how best to en-gage them and become proficient at making their experience with you memorable. This does not mean pandering. Even antagonists turn up to my talks, if only as agent provocateurs. Recall what I said in the previous chapter: people do not remember what they hear but what they feel. To be sure that the audience feels something, treat them as participants in the performance. A participant plays a role. This is the quickest and most effective way of enhancing your performance.

In the following chapter, I detail techniques that I adopt to in-volve the audience. What I describe is far more useful than the oft-repeated practice of asking audiences about their familiarity with the topic, to introduce themselves, or whether they're enjoying the experience. These questions are valid, but not during your perfor-mance. The moment you ask the audience to share something about themselves is the moment you lose control. Instead, be clever about involving them in a way that complements your performance. To involve your audience, you must pay attention and learn to read them. Staring at your notes or your feet, looking past them, or turn-ing your back while commenting on your slides will deprive you of vital information. You cannot observe how they are receiving your performance, preventing any real-time adaptations. The techniques below will help you achieve more lively performances, by trans-forming the experience from passive to proactive.

*

INVOLVING YOUR AUDIENCE

Involving the audience takes many forms, though the most common role is that of witness. Participants observe and the speaker invites them to answer questions during the performance. Using questions to provoke reflection and engagement is a standard public speaking technique. Yet, regardless of the audience, this endeavour mostly ends in failure. Unless you call on individuals directly, few people are bold enough to speak out in public. First, audience members are fearful of embarrassing themselves so will mostly stay quiet. Second, questions trigger the 'Hermione' effect, as a handful of individuals relish the opportunity to answer all questions. Third, since the answer to a question is fleeting and solitary, it produces only superficial levels of participation.

Instead of treating your audience like a gaggle of witnesses, visualise an orchestra sitting before you: the audience is reading from the same music sheet with each contributing in their own way. In the best circumstances, an orchestra achieves a symphony; in the worst, they produce a cacophony. The metaphor also represents the speaker as conductor, whose role is to coordinate the skills of others. Some speakers take issue with this, perceiving themselves as more active than a maestro. The criticism is accurate, and the metaphor does not quite fit. I am drawing your attention to the collaborative nature of the exercise and to the contribution each member of the audience makes. Stated otherwise, it is your role to cajole a group of individuals to work collaboratively and to produce something harmonious. What I mean by this and how you achieve it will become clearer as the sub-sections unfold.

FACIAL EXPRESSIONS

My favourite audience members are the expressive ones. They have difficulty hiding their emotions and respond to my statements with effusive grimaces. Each expression provides an opportunity for engagement, and I routinely probe them on it. Here are some examples:

- 'Your frown tells me you do not agree. Is it the argument or the evidence that you doubt?'
- 'I am pleased to see you smiling. What just became clearer?'
- 'Ms X, what part of my explanation is troubling you?'

Treat your audience's expressions as both information and opportunity. By reading their expressions, you will better understand how they are receiving your performance. Such information is invaluable as it tells you much about the clarity and persuasiveness of your exposition. Their expressions also provide you with countless prompts for engagement. While attendees might still feel anxious, you make the task easier by soliciting reflections on their reactions rather than answers to questions they are ill-prepared for.

QUESTIONS

Readers often misinterpret my earlier remarks as a prohibition on interrogating your audience. This is not the case. What matters is the type of question posed and the type of answer solicited. Questions you should avoid are those that query their familiarity with the topic or materials (you should know this based on your audience's composition); about their personality or mood ('how is everyone feeling today?'); about life's meaning (both literally and metaphorically); and about almost all things personal, but especially their parents, their children, their faith, or any traumatic experiences. There are others, but these suffice to buttress my point.

Any good barrister knows not to ask a question they do not already know the answer to. While this rule is impracticable in most settings outside a courtroom, the underlying rationale is relevant: if you do not know what a witness will say, do not ask as their response could derail your argument or, worse, your case. Public speakers should avoid posing questions that will undermine their performance. In almost all cases, the categories of questions enumerated above will add nothing meaningful to your performance. Instead, be tactical with the questions and only ask those that complement your performance.

Simplified to a granular level, distinguish between two types of questions: closed and open. Closed questions demand concise answers, for they present respondents with limited options. They are most useful in warming the audience up. Examples are abundant: have you ever owned a pet? Do you holiday abroad often? What did you study at university? I use closed questions as precursors to open ones.

As per the label, open questions allow for creativity and variation. The most skilled barristers can pose open questions that appear closed and vice versa. Leading questions are the most common: the questions point the respondent towards the answer. What made your performance so exhilarating? Did you stumble over the question because you cannot remember what happened or because you are embellishing your answer? Next are recall questions. While asking someone to recall information might seem like a closed question, remember what I explained earlier: we forget the vast majority of what we hear shortly after hearing it. Recall questions help jog our memory, yes, but they also create new narratives and thus generate additional information. Much depends on how you phrase it. For example, 'What do you recall about your last birthday?' is not as effective as, 'What about your previous birthday stood out?' The latter allows for more editorialising, thus yielding higher degrees of involvement.

Do not confuse recall questions with process questions, for the latter require more analysis and critique. For example, 'Would a higher budget help this department increase productivity?' demands that the respondent reflect both on the department and the two additional variables: budget and productivity. While this could be an invaluable question in soliciting different viewpoints, its complexity means that a speaker must allocate time for participants to prepare answers. Funnelling questions can help speed up reflection on a process question. Instead of leaving them to their own devices, closed and leading questions funnel the respondent towards a specific form of analysis. Consider the following illustration where I substitute my previous process question with a funnelling series.

1. Do higher budgets normally help or hinder
   a department's development?
   Answer: help
2. What about a higher budget is helpful to the department?
   Answer: they can use the budget to hire 'better staff'
3. How do 'better staff' enhance a department's
   functionality or productivity?
   Answer: ...

By asking a series of questions like this, I lead my audience towards a specific outcome while leaving them with the impression that they processed the information autonomously. Along the way, I increase support for the underlying sentiment.

I left rhetorical questions for last. As per their appellation, rhetorical questions provoke. Done well, they add value. They can be humorous or controversial, two sentiments that stimulate. However, since the point is not to answer them, use these sparingly lest it become a mundane device that the audience glosses over.

Questions have layers and can be effective tools for engaging the audience and evaluating your performance. More often than not, the speaker squanders the opportunity by asking the wrong type of question, thus soliciting a hotchpotch of answers, many of which are unhelpful to their performance.

ANSWERS

Answers are as complex as questions and provide another window through which you can involve your audience. Learning about common types of answers will help you improve your ability to ask questions. It will also help you adapt to the dynamic shifts that occur in oral performances. Here, I detail six types of answers you can expect from your audiences.

Direct and complete answers are ideal. The respondent stays on point and provides a comprehensive answer to the query posed. You should respond in three ways. First, reward the respondent: I do this by acknowledging the quality of the answer, asking the audience to applaud their peer, or writing it up if I have a board behind me. Validation encourages repeat behaviour. Second, ask someone else to comment on the answer delivered. By circulating the responses among others, you deepen rapport within the group. Third, build upon it. Quality answers are not precious artefacts to memorialise but raw material to develop. Use these answers to your advantage by merging them with your speech.

Partial answers are self-explanatory: the respondent only goes part way. Whether they did so out of uncertainty or laziness is irrelevant. Our task is to help them—and the others—to complete the trajectory. Highlighting the incompleteness will only discourage others from answering future questions. The trick is to probe them on what they said and to use either funnelling or leading questions to tease out the rest. Funnelling questions are ideal in situations where you wish to draw out the analysis (this is useful for students), while leading questions are apt when the desired answer is key (such as during witness examinations or a funding pitch to an angel fund). Like direct answers, merge partial ones with the overall speech.

Perhaps counter-intuitively, one of the easiest types of answer to capitalise on is the incorrect one. Despite any disappointment we might feel about our ineffective communication of information, an incorrect answer is almost a blessing. It is a do-over. I respond to an incorrect answer with phrases such as 'I seem to have skipped a part of my argument'; 'That was unexpected; let's examine where our paths diverged'; and, 'I had not thought of that. Let's try this again'. Regardless of how you respond, your aim is to validate the respondent while using the opportunity to recap the underlying analysis. When asking again, I infer the answer while explaining why the respondent answered as they did.

The next type is what I term out-of-context or out-to-lunch answers. Public speakers soon realise that what we say and what the audience hears can be light years apart. As a result, respondents make statements unconnected to our topic or irrelevant to our question. This places us in a bind. If we let it slide, we risk confusing our audience. If we highlight the irrelevance, we risk alienating the respondent, not to mention the rest of the audience who will not want to embarrass themselves either. What to do?

I approach out-of-context answers as genuine but misguided attempts at participation. The individual means well, even if they do not quite get it. I respond in one of three ways, all of which are effective in enhancing their understanding. I encourage you to rotate between them. First, I paraphrase and reformulate their answer to advance my argument. Rarely, if ever, am I challenged on this. On the contrary, they are pleased to have contributed. Second, I reformulate their answer to force a link between it and my question. I then ask them to expand on a specific point I just made. My second approach is higher risk as, in essence, I am asking them to double down on what they said. Third, I acknowledge their answer, again in my own words, before shelving it. I do this either by telling them I will return to it later or that discussing this answer would steer us too far from the topic at hand. This is the least desirable approach, and I reserve it for audience members who intervene too often.

Out-to-lunch answers are more problematic as they are not merely off course but outside the topic. In these instances, there is sufficient evidence to question the respondent's motivation: they might wish to disrupt or, and this happens, are unstable. Once I classify the individual as either, my preferred tactic is to avoid eye contact. This can be effective, but can also make you uncomfortable and thus disturb your performance. Another approach is to use curt replies to minimise the disruption: 'Thank you for that interesting point'; 'Very good. I get to that later'; and 'That is a little off topic'. Other attendees understand what you are doing, even if the respondent does not and are usually sympathetic to your plight. Use the audience to your advantage by calling on them. Disruptive or unstable audience members are now common at public events, and you should prepare for the inevitable.

Empty answers are another common response. Two forms prevail: guessing and waffling. The stimulus for both is identical: insecurity or overconfidence. Nervous of appearing ill-prepared or ignorant, the respondent fabricates an answer (which they deliver with great hesitation). It is almost always a guess intended solely to bring their anxiety to an end. Wafflers, on the other hand, ramble. Their nerves have gotten the better of them, stymying any form of structure to their response, or they enjoy hearing themselves speak and believe others will enjoy their wisdom.

Those who guess are only participating because we demand it. Otherwise, they would remain quiet. I used to ask these types how they got to their answer before repeated blank stares convinced me to deal with them differently. My approach is slightly more assertive now. I call out their guesses before encouraging them to try again, this time making an educated guess. They can use some information to eliminate wrong answers and then choose the best option that remains. With insecure wafflers, I ask them to synthesise their response into a single sentence and then praise them (sincerely) for their brevity. For conceited wafflers, I ask another member of the audience what they took away from the response. I then ask if this is what they meant and, if not, to provide us with a single sentence synthesis.

While empty answers can frustrate, more often than not, they provide useful feedback. They communicate that the audience does not understand us or is not paying attention. It is useful information, even if it stings.

By far the most common type of answer is the last one on my list: silence. Anyone who has spoken in public knows that the vast majority of your audience will look towards the ceiling, their shoes, into the distance, or just anywhere other than your direction when you ask a question. Silence is a formidable foe which can throw off even the most experienced speakers. What does silence convey: that the audience is not listening, confused, or disinterested? It could also mean that you have transfixed them with your performance. Or maybe they are daydreaming? There's the rub: since the audience stays silent, we cannot know. This explains the speed at which doubt takes hold of a speaker. Three strategies help break the logjam.

First, I present the audience with a general question that I want them to reflect upon and answer internally. Within ten to fifteen seconds, I ask them to share their answer with the person next to them. Following this, I outline some answers offered in a previous lecture, suggesting that these might have come up. The second time I do this, I ask them to raise their hands if their answer is on my list. By the third time, I ask them to volunteer their answers. Trial runs, where audience members speak to one another, provide them with an opportunity to build their confidence before sharing anything collectively. The exercise is a warm-up that leaves your audience a little more limber and willing.

My second technique involves asking a question and then volunteering answers. I explain each in turn. I then ask which arguments are most convincing and what makes them more convincing than the others. Fear of volunteering the wrong answer is more paralysing than fear of speaking your mind. By asking the audience to explain what they find most convincing rather than what is most convincing, we put them at ease, making them more amenable to participating.

My ultimate technique for involving silent audiences is, I admit, opportunistic. Instead of leaving it to chance, I build rapport with my audience before the talk begins. I mentioned this in Chapter 7. Familiarising yourself with the audience breaks down several barriers. They come to understand you as personable. These few individuals you befriend now feel a slight sense of solidarity with you. While you cannot rely upon them to answer all questions, they will intervene when the going gets tough. This technique has bailed me out on plenty of occasions. After posing the question, I turn to the familiar faces and hold their gaze longer than usual. Cynical, perhaps, but I am not above guilting audience members into helping me deliver a more engaging speech, and you should not be either.

Just as you can read the facial expressions of your audience or tailor your questions to create a more involved atmosphere, so too does probing your audience's answers help you better understand them. With greater understanding, comes greater ability: you can reform an attendee who waffles just as you can guide one who delivers a partial answer. All answers require some engagement from the speaker, so they better serve the performance. Recall what I said at the outset: just as you do not ask questions to solicit information, you should not treat answers as anything more than another tool in your performance.

USING THEIR MATERIALS

Another simple way to build rapport with your audience is to use their materials. At oral performances, most attendees will have at least: a pen, a piece of paper, and a phone. A few more will have water bottles, keys, and perhaps a backpack, purse, or satchel. For the purpose of involving the audience, all items are fair game.

The act is mundane, but the effect is potent. Request the item and inject it into your discussion. Your use of the item should be casual and always to illustrate a simple point, making it easy to remember. I have used a pen to show the law of gravity, a blank page to exemplify how all brilliant ideas begin, and a mobile phone to explain how conceptions of privacy are evolving. Again, notice how basic the points are. I do not use their items to generate an epiphany. Chances are most attendees already understand how gravity works.

The aim is to integrate the audience into the performance. It strengthens ties with the speaker as those in attendance become part of the performance. Whether they expected it or even wanted it, your performance enshrouds them. Henceforth, whenever the item reappears, they will recall its use in your performance and reflect on the speech. This is a facile but powerful use of mnemonics.

While there is no hard and fast rule, my aim is to make use of audience materials two to three times during my performance and, in repeat lectures (at universities), to target a range of attendees and spread the playfulness far and wide.

*

The audience is neither your enemy nor your friend: the audience is part of the performance. Amateur and professional speakers alike misunderstand this point, keeping the audience several arms' lengths away or embracing them as though they were family (I recently read a tweet from a colleague declaring that they wanted to be 'vulnerable' with their students). I regard both approaches as flawed.

I return to my orchestra metaphor: you are the conductor, the maestro. You instigate the performance; you set the tone; and you solicit contributions. Facial expressions, questions, answers, and even materials are conduits to involving your audience. There are others, of course. I have seen speakers ask audience members to recap key points or to use their smartphone to research a definition. Each tactic is valid, and there are others you can explore.

A conductor appreciates that a symphony is more harmonious when all musicians feel the experience. For example, in December 2019, the Paris Opera Orchestra went on strike. They held an impromptu performance on the steps of the Opera House and in front of thousands of fellow trade unionists and citizens. It would be hokey to describe the experience as magical but, according to the conductor, he never experienced greater harmony. Common causes unite. Camaraderie between the maestro, musicians, and the audience stimulated synergy between the participants. We can emulate their example. Pay close attention to your audience, for your performance will live and die by their response to it. Your reputation will as well.

14

DRAWING ON THE CHARACTERS IN YOUR STORY

In Chapter 8, I unpacked the popularity of Ted Talks. In a nutshell, Ted speakers couch performances in stories. Across the human species, stories form the basis of communication and education. By deploying the narrative model, Ted Talks tap into our sociological development. The point goes deeper than this. It is not that our lives consist of stories, but that our lives are stories. It is impossible to understand our existence without them.

Stories showcase an array of components including: characters, controversies, crescendos, emotions, and plots. Each is essential, though characters take the trophy. I dedicate a full chapter to characters as their influence over a performance is second only to that of the audience.

We associate characters with status: they are protagonists. The examples are countless: Tutankhamun, Julius Caesar, Romeo and Juliet, Kunta Kinte, and Toussaint L'Ouverture. The success of fiction and non-fiction stories is contingent on a well-developed character who intrigues and provokes in equal measure. Their adventures ensnare us, their quirks captivate us, and their personalities enthral us. Each protagonist makes the story come alive and, when we recall Star Wars, we think more about Darth Vader, Luke Skywalker, and Yoda than we do about the Death Star, light sabers, or the Millennium Falcon. All three objects are critical to the plot, but we rarely afford them more than a cursory thought. Yoda, however, is timeless.

Equally important to these stories are George Lucas (director of Star Wars), Shakespeare (his reputation precedes him), and CLR James (author of an autobiography on Toussaint L'Ouverture). While it is sensible to develop the protagonists of a story, it is also sensible to account for the contributory value of the supporting cast. Implications for the speaker are many as they must adopt an expansive definition of characters to acknowledge the contribution of the supporting cast. This means accounting for yourself, your audience, and anyone else of import to your story. Let me provide an example.

One of my earliest trials involved the CEO of an important company. We represented the company in most of their transactions and litigation. Because of an unfortunate twist of events, the CEO asked us, as a personal favour, to draft the separation agreement between him and his spouse. A family law specialist would have been more appropriate, but the partner responsible for the account decided we should lend a hand. There was a catch, however: the CEO wanted us to include a clause by which the spouse agreed to forfeit all future child support payments for a lump sum payout. Lawyers reading this book will immediately spot the minefield: these clauses run against public order and thus unenforceable. Why? Parents recognise their joint accountability for their offspring and pay their share of the costs, irrespective of custodial arrangements. It was clear the CEO wished to avoid this.

I advised the CEO of what I just explained. If the matter ended up before a judge, opposing counsel would take us apart for trying to pull a fast one. The former spouse's lawyer and the representative of the child would highlight the illegality of our action, and wax hyperbolically about the wealth of the CEO. His lifestyle would be on the agenda, as would supermarket expenses. Even a second-rate lawyer would take us to the cleaners as the agreement infers that the CEO is an opportunist, willing to fleece his former family despite the considerable wealth he possessed. I advised the CEO that we would lose because there was no effective way to dispute the characterisation without besmirching the two victims. A risk taker, the CEO (and partner) insisted that we proceed. The outcome was a costly foregone conclusion for, in this story, the characters' backstories were too relatable, too emotive, and too powerful. Even if I could account for the protagonists—for example by digging up dirt on the former spouse to hold the child liable for their parent's misdeeds—the other characters of the story lined up against us.

My long-winded illustration should clarify that, despite the centrality of protagonists, public speakers must also account for the other characters in the story. For me, this means reflecting on how I develop my backstory, tease out or infer the backstory of audience members, and develop the backstories of anyone else of relevance to my speech. This perhaps sounds more complicated than it is and so, in the rest of this chapter, I describe how it works in practice.

THE PROTAGONIST

You are an essential character in your performance, not only because you are the maestro but because you are under the microscope. I explained this in Chapter 5: audiences dissect public speakers to a granular level. It is not that skilled public speakers razzle and dazzle, shifting the audience's focus away from them. Rather, skilled public speakers integrate themselves into the performance, becoming part of the story.

Those familiar with the film director, Quentin Tarantino, have an advantage here. From his earliest films, Tarantino has cast himself in strategic roles. When queried, he pontificated about the benefits of seeing the production through both sides of the lens. He is no longer just the director, shooting the film as puppet master. By integrating himself, he alters the experience of the other actors and of the audience. Acting provides him with a more rounded perspective of his film, and it with a deeper appreciation of his commitment to the production. Again, those who've watched his films understand more about his personality because his character grows from picture to picture. The gains for Tarantino are immense as he makes himself and his films more memorable.

This is true for a public speaker. By developing yourself during your performances, the audience will appreciate you more. It is not about what you share, but that you do share. To be clear, this tactic does not conflict with my previous warning about the audience not being your friend (Chapter 16). You are not sharing information to befriend your audience, but to make yourself more memorable. Statements such as 'This reminds me of a crack squash player I was up against last week'; 'During a layover in Havana…'; and 'Unlike my brother, the computer engineer in the family…'. Each of these mini revelations humanises you before your audience, helping them answer some questions they have about you. Think of yourself as a blank slate: listening to a blank slate is jarring. By peppering your performance with personal titbits, you develop your character and deepen your appeal.

THE AUDIENCE

An under-used character in most public performances is the audience. Some dispute this claim. They argue that public speakers probe the audience during their performance or the Q&A afterward. Is this not involving your audience? It is, but a Q&A engages individual members of the audience. I refer to treating the audience as a character in their own right.

Recall occasions where you walked into a room and felt it teeming with energy. The room and the crowd generate a buzz that invigorates us. Contrast this sentiment with the one you felt when walking into a chilly room. Perhaps the audience is quiet; perhaps they are sitting far apart; and perhaps it is wet and windy outside. Regardless, we notice the distance instantly as the chill saps our energy. In those moments, you feel the character of the audience.

It is difficult to explain why the character of a group develops the way it does. I mentioned some factors above, but there are others. We cannot account for each factor, and thus cannot know. Regardless, audiences possess a collective character that will influence how your performance pans out. Reflecting on this character provides important information that you can deploy to your advantage.

Let me begin with an example. As I mentioned in the preface, I have spoken in many parts of the world and have learned to appreciate that audiences differ according to social norms. The lecture I gave in Bogota to a room full of legal practitioners was lively, not because I made it so but because Colombians—like many South American—are more exuberant, even among the conservative professional elite. On offer were facial expressions galore, loud laughter, and even sporadic applause that warmed the heart and spirit. Contrast this with the lecture I delivered to a similar group in Beijing. Foreigners who travel to China are often perplexed by the distinct social norms. Provoking laughter is possible, but you are more likely to plateau around subtle mirth. Interruptions are non-existent. Even the applause feels prosaic. Do not misunderstand me: many of my Chinese friends have a joie de vivre that dwarfs that of my Colombian ones. The difference is in the way they express it. The Chinese are more muted. I recall taking a photo with the Dean and Deputy Dean (and their assistants) at a major Chinese law school. Flatteringly, I am positioned at the centre of our group of five. Unflatteringly, I am grinning like a Cheshire cat while the others appear as sombre as pallbearers. Who looks the fool? I learned that smiling in the way I did with the Colombian practitioners is awkward within a Chinese context. Knowing the culture of your audience, which can be as distinct as my Bogota and Beijing experiences, will help you adjust to their character and allow you to make them more comfortable.

Alongside culture is context. Again, an example will help. The New Zealand Office of Ethnic Affairs invited me to deliver a speech about the rights of children. While this is innocuous in its own right, they upped the ante: they instigated the event following an Israeli bombing campaign that killed scores of Palestinian children and it was taking place at a church—St-Matthew-in-the-City—known for its progressive politics. With context in mind, I prepared accordingly. Since I was speaking at a church, I could expect the audience to be primarily elderly, hopeful, and pious. In addition, the venue would add an air of solemnity to the occasion. Finally, the subtext of the topic was the suffering and salvation of children, hardly material for a barn-burning speech. These factors combined to create a distinct context that I had to account for.

Ability to account for character, culture, and context comes with preparation. I often inject the distinctiveness of these three elements into my introduction, as a gag about raising my cultural awareness or about the impossible order the organisers tasked me with. However you do it, your aim is to share with your audience the awareness you possess and how you have adapted your speech. Building upon these nuances will yield a deeper connection, as you convey to them their importance.

YOUR STORY'S CHARACTERS

In the previous subsections, I encouraged you to think expansively about characters: both you and your audience are characters who you can integrate into the performance. Also at your disposal are many others, each of whom is crying out for some characterisation. I begin my explanation with a passage from a text I often reference when training speakers:

"It happened on April 19, 1964. It was bluebell time in Kent. Mr. and Mrs. Hinz had been married some 10 years, and they had four children, all aged nine and under. The youngest was one. Mrs. Hinz was a remarkable woman. In addition to her own four, she was foster-mother to four other children. To add to it, she was two months pregnant with her fifth child."

It will surprise many to hear that this is the opening paragraph of a Court of Appeal judgment delivered in 1970: Hinz v Berry [1967 H. No 95] (the full text is available online). It reads like a work of fiction. But what we are told in the subsequent paragraph provoked judge Denning, a well-regarded and conservative member of the Court of Appeal bench, to break from convention.

"On this day they drove out in a Bedford Dormobile van from Tonbridge to Canvey Island. They took all eight children with them. As they were coming back, they turned into a lay-by at Thurnham to have a picnic tea. The husband, Mr. Hinz, was at the back of the Dormobile making the tea. Mrs. Hinz had taken Stephanie, her third child, aged three, across the road to pick bluebells on the opposite side. There came along a Jaguar car driven by Mr. Berry, out of control. A tyre had burst. The Jaguar rushed into this lay-by and crashed into Mr. Hinz and the children. Mr. Hinz was frightfully injured and died a little later. Nearly all the children were hurt. Blood was streaming from their heads. Mrs. Hinz, hearing the crash, turned round and saw the disaster. She ran across the road and did all she could. Her husband was beyond recall. But the children recovered."

Denning's overtures to Mrs. Hinz are deliberate. The judge is tugging at our heartstrings. She is a remarkable woman, pregnant with her fifth child, and mother to four foster children (I accept that some would regard this praise as patriarchal, but Denning was a man of his time). She is responsible, rushing to the scene to care for the wounded. She is caring, picking flowers with her three-year-old. What happens next is difficult, not just for the late Mrs. Hinz, but also for the readers: the Court of Appeal rules against her claim. Denning uses this sympathetic character description to demolish her appeal—and that of future claimants—for remedies for grief and sorrow.

"In English law no damages are awarded for grief or sorrow caused by a person's death. No damages are to be given for the worry about the children, or the financial strain or stress, or the difficulties of adjusting to a new life. Damages are, however, recoverable for nervous shock, or, to put it in medical terms, for any recognisable psychiatric illness caused by the breach of duty by the defendant."

Denning then declares that the qualities Mrs. Hinz possesses, those he celebrated earlier, made her "a woman of great capacity." He opined that she would have gotten over the loss of her husband "in say, a year."

Most law students remember this case because of the devastating outcome for Mrs. Hinz and the brutality of both law and court, a reality that bursts any misconceptions they had about law as a pathway to justice. What junior barristers learn is that characters are critical to developing a persuasive narrative. The contours of a story are easier to recall when we situate characters at its core. Our ability to connect to them, stimulates our senses and our attention.

When I tell the story of Mrs. Hinz, I also paint a portrait of Denning. Denning's character is essential in understanding his perception of the law. We have no reason to doubt his sincerity towards the plight of Mrs. Hinz. However, he proves his commitment to a narrow interpretation of the law of remedies by his willingness to dismiss his sympathy for her plight. As he implies in the concluding paragraph, a true jurist motivated by justice could do nothing else. I describe Denning in depth as his conservatism informs his perception of the law and even blinds him to the bias inherent in his own interpretation. For example, in one part of the judgment he praises the insurance company for their conscientiousness. Do readers of the judgment remember this? Probably not. But what they remember is that Denning could, with the stoicism of granite, send a woman and her children to the poorhouse because justice demands no less. Because of the story, the performance is captivating; the characters make the point memorable.

*

As I explained in this chapter's introduction, stories consist of characters. They are also full of details about landscapes, plots, and outfits. What stays with us, what we tell our friends and family about over dinner, are the characters: who they are, how they behave, and what we think of them. This makes sense. It is far easier for us to relate to people than it is for us to connect with a sand dune, no matter how skilful the narrator is. Once the narrator describes the sand, sun, and sweat, we immediately imagine the character—or ideally ourselves—suffocating under the weight of the swelter. Despite our natural affinity for characters, most public performances place inordinate weight on information, devoid of personalities. This is a flawed approach. Characters act as mnemonics that the audience will remember: whether it is you mimicking the voice of Marlon Brando as Don Corleone, or painting a picture of William Churchill as a drunk and a bigot (he was both). Characters are associative devices that help us remember things. Paint them well.

15

FRAMING FOR COHERENCE AND CLARITY

A key weakness of many public performances is the speaker's failure to outline the frame. Frame is not context. A failure to set the context is another flaw, but not the one I discuss here. A frame delineates a speech within the confines of the debate that the speech relates to. It is essential not only to situate yourself in relation to other experts on your topic, but also to position yourself within the topic itself. To use an easy example, throughout this text I refer to other public speaking coaches. I also distinguish between distinct styles of public speaking, setting out the aim of this book: to help readers develop their performative skills. I clarify that it is an introductory text that covers basic and advanced techniques, to help make the practitioner more captivating and memorable. If a reader wishes to be more authentic or passionate, they should read another book.

There is no flippancy in my statement. This book contains next to nothing about authenticity or passion. Why? First, that is not how I approach public speaking and, second, these themes fall outside the contours of this book. Are authenticity and passion relevant to public speaking? Undoubtedly. But neither an author nor a book can cover all themes within a topic, making it essential that I frame my position within the field. Framing helps mediate the expectations of the audience: if you promise your audience the world and only deliver Southeast Asia, they will feel short-changed. If you promise them Southeast Asia with an acknowledgement that you will mostly speak about Indonesia, Malaysia, and Singapore and extrapolate wider conclusions about the region from these three case studies, your position is firmer.

For your audience, a framed topic is an accessible topic. By honing in on a specific topic rather than, say, pontificating across topics, your audience is better able to keep up. You have provided them with a map of the African continent and identified Cairo as your point of departure and Khartoum as your point of arrival. They see the continent and situate your trajectory in relation to the wider geography, but it does not distract them. In communications and in media training, they often term this 'message discipline'. A speaker should stay on point, avoiding digressions or tangents and personal quips that distract from the core message. For a public speaker who wishes to be captivating, message discipline is not what you are pursuing. To you, it is about positioning your speech within the wider debate to help the audience navigate the morass.

There is authenticity in framing: you do what you say you will. More important for our purposes, however, is the impact that framing has on your audience, your performance, and your ability to signal. Let's explore this last element in more detail.

WHAT IS SIGNALLING?

For a public speaker, signals act as beacons or homing devices: by repeating signals to the audience, you help keep them on the same trajectory. We intersperse keywords or phrases across our speech to bolster the audience's awareness of the direction and the relation to the wider topic. I hinted at this in Chapter 6, where I spoke about sharing the lesson and structure with the audience at the outset. Signals go a little further than the outline, however. For example, in the previous section I reiterated an earlier point about the book: that I am not teaching you to be authentic or passionate. Repeat references help the audience remain on the same track.

You may have noticed other signals: references to previous chapters, the aim of being captivating and memorable, and the type of learning that I target. Each of these signals situates my thinking in relation to that other practitioners and highlights pathways towards your improvement. Using management language, signals are nudges.

My favourite metaphor for signalling is that of a sheepdog. Anyone who has seen a sheepdog in action knows that they are discrete, quiet, and effective. They can move a herd of beasts with no ballyhoo. They nudge at the fringes to keep them on track. A sheepdog, like a competent public speaker, understands that there is an origin and a destination, and a trajectory between these two points. All the previous techniques provide you with the ability to capture the herd's attention. However, keeping their attention, holding them together, and moving them along the itinerary is more complicated. The sheepdog stealthily nudges them in the right direction. You should do the same with signals.

HOW TO SIGNAL?

I practice signalling in four ways, all of which build upon the practice of framing discussed in the intro to this chapter. In the first two techniques, I use words and concepts common to the topic. I quote from an article about intellectual property to explain an ideal approach. The passage sets out the frame within which the authors proceed.

"We locate our approach to the history of intellectual property within a critical framework, distinguishing it from what Robert Cox has referred to as problem-solving approaches. In particular, we present our account as an alternative to both functionalist and realist treatments of such a history. We seek to demonstrate the utility of a critical perspective, which unlike realism, is agnostic about the primary actors and can suggest links between the micro and macro levels. Realism provides limited leverage in the intellectual property context as private actors, rather than states, have frequently prompted changes in intellectual property protection. Thus while realism takes power seriously, it suffers from its statist (institutionalist) orientation, treating the state as a broadly unitary actor with well-defined interests.

*

In light of such tendencies, below we present selected turning points in the development of the institution of intellectual property to illuminate the persistent tension between those who seek to privately appropriate property in intellectual goods and those who seek its dissemination."

This is a piece of academic prose and inappropriate in a public performance. However, if we look past the text's inaccessibility, we have a fine example of framing: the authors situate their analysis within the wider debate. They will examine:

- The history of intellectual property
- Within a critical framework
- But not a problem-solving framework
- And distinguishing from a realist approach
  (that overemphasises the state)
- To illuminate tension between the purpose of intellectual property as capture and as a practice of dissemination

Whether you understand the implications of their analysis is irrelevant. By framing their text with such clarity and precision, they have pinpointed a series of signals they can use throughout a presentation. History as a signal is obvious; it is the centre of their passage. Historical accounts are always controversial and they can exploit points of difference to situate themselves. This is true of the critical framework. It provides a lens through which to understand their speech in much the same way that the problem-solving and realist approaches do. They tell us that their critique is distinct from these other approaches which the audience members should understand. Signalling the competing frameworks will enhance the audience's ability to remain engaged in the performance.

The final useful signal for our academic authors is the kicker: the tension between the aims of intellectual property. Even those with rudimentary knowledge of intellectual property appreciate that it is a model of proprietary rights that facilitates rent seeking by the owner of the intellectual work, whether a film, a brand, or an invention. Users of the work must get a license from the owner to engage in an array of activities including broadcasting a film, designing shirts that bear the brand, or integrating an invention into another. In contrast, the authors infer an alternative aim: disseminating intellectual works widely. Those familiar with the debate understand that this phrase references the public domain, itself a layered and nuanced concept. The controversy is clear, fashioning a canal down which they can funnel the speech. For the speakers, the walls of this canal provide concrete materials for signalling. Whether referencing capture or dissemination, each concept will help the audience follow the logic of the argument. In this way, the debate and the concepts that comprise the debate provide fertile ground for effective signalling.

The third and fourth signal types involve other individuals relevant to your speech and their relationship to you. Return to the passage I quoted above and re-read the first sentence. In this single sentence, the authors provide no less than four potential signals: 1) The history of intellectual property (previously mentioned); 2) A critical framework; 3) Robert Cox; and 4) Problem-solving approaches. Since the authors are writing for an expert audience, they can get away with this level of specificity. Regardless, even the most competent and engaged attendees will become distracted as the speech unfolds (I have already spoken at length about the difficulties audiences face). By referencing another scholar and their approach in the opening sentence, the authors have another useful signal at their disposal.

Here, the 'other relevant person' is a fellow academic who offers a competing approach to the topic. Recall the purchase of personalities: by portraying your relationship to another scholar, the audience is more capable of connecting the dots. Seeing the two approaches side by side, the picture becomes clearer and more vibrant. It is common knowledge that critics approach the same subjects from distinct angles: both a Libertarian and Marxist might lament the state of a country's regulatory regime, but they do so for contrasting reasons. Signalling the arguments of others will add greater heft to your performance.

The value of signals lies, first, in their ability to create a conduit through which you can guide your audience. Second, is their potential for bolstering your credibility. You showcase yourself as being in command not only of your performance but also of the field itself.

*

From a very early age, I developed the habit of observing my surroundings. This resulted from both my personality and my upbringing. My parents moved us from city to city and, in each one, would gift me a bicycle. I always had an affinity for two wheels, and my parents nurtured this love affair (to their great chagrin when I rolled up on my first Ducati). In each city, I left in the morning and returned when hunger struck. I rode my bike everywhere: from suburbs to central stations, on back roads and overpasses alike. It remains my favourite mode of travel and you can often catch me exploring an unknown city on a rental.

One thing that stands out about my riding is that I never get lost, regardless of my familiarity with the city. This is odd and I often wonder if it is the chicken or the egg: does navigating come easily to me because it does or because I spent countless hours riding unknown streets and learning the tricks of navigation? Key to my proficiency is identifying landmarks and reading signals: high rises, parks, hills, and roads. There is nothing unique in this: all navigators and trackers map their surroundings, in real-time, when exploring. Contrary to what many believe, it is much less about reading tea leaves than it is about noticing the obvious. Since landmarks will never move, we can always rely upon them to provide our location: they act as a frame we move within. When we add to this the signals—for example, traffic flows into the city in the morning and out in the evening—we can determine whether we are on the right path.

Landmarks and signals are the responsibility of the speaker. You set the frame and plot the trajectory. To ensure that the audience remains on the path, you provide them with signals, which also help them check back in if they veer off course. Signalling is an advanced technique that takes time to master. If you begin by practising framing, you quickly realise that a frame works best when complemented by an array of signals. Frames reinforce signals and signals reinforce frames: as you learn to develop them, they will learn to read them. Neither you nor your audience will ever get lost again.

16

IN LIEU OF A CONCLUSION

Congratulations! You have reached the end of the book. Learning something new fires the synapses, triggering novel connections and creating fertile conditions for personal growth. Frame is not context. A failure to set the context is another flaw, but not the one I discuss here. A frame delineates a speech within the confines of the debate that the speech relates to. It is essential not only to situate yourself in relation to other experts on your topic, but also to position yourself within the topic itself. To use an easy example, throughout this text I refer to other public speaking coaches. I also distinguish between distinct styles of public speaking, setting out the aim of this book: to help readers develop their performative skills. I clarify that it is an introductory text that covers basic and advanced techniques, to help make the practitioner more captivating and memorable. If a reader wishes to be more authentic or passionate, they should read another book.

Psychologists term this the snowball effect for momentum begets momentum. In this chapter, I provide some essential reflections about public speaking.

I would not be who I am if it were not for the education others provided, many unbeknownst to them. These teachings have brought me splendid success in public speaking and beyond. The greatest lesson I gained is knowledge that the skills needed to be captivating and memorable are hidden in plain sight. Education is everywhere: this book, YouTube, or the next event you attend. Bad public speaking does not result from lack of knowledge but lack of effort. What differentiates speakers is the quality of the knowledge they possess and the effort they make (that others avoid).

You are one of those individuals willing to improve your public speaking skills by having read this book. The reflections I include below are for you. They are little kernels that I gained over the years and that I share with those willing to listen. Each reflection enjoys the same unenviable quality: a moment of disappointment sparked them. Yet, despite the discomfort that these moments precipitated, they remain a source of learning both about the craft and about the self.

My disappointments taught me much and, if you pursue what I outline in this book, you will experience similar moments. What I hope is that my reflections will soften the blow and encourage you to trudge on. Indeed, if there is one thing I am sure of in this life, it is the importance of perseverance, as those who do not keep trying are inevitably forgotten.

NO HAPPY ENDINGS

In 2019, I travelled to Edmonton to lecture on legal pedagogy to staff at the University of Alberta. The organisers asked me to speak about the ubiquitous student engagement problem. As many of you will learn, keeping audiences awake sometimes supersedes the challenge of keeping them engaged. Professors fare even worse. Not only do the students wish they were elsewhere, but they are not mature enough to keep quiet. Their displeasure comes at us through the barrel of a bullhorn.

As I highlighted earlier, I used the spaghetti western motif as a backdrop for the speech, which I entitled The Magnificent Seven of Academic Lecturing. You will recognise some techniques I spoke to: crescendos, predictable plot lines, and slow delivery. My seventh technique, however, set the room ablaze. I concluded by telling the audience that, despite their best efforts, there would be no happy endings. You could feel the room implode once the phrase dropped. It was a sucker punch. These academics turned up committed and eager, and I rewarded them with a bag of sick.

This was one of my first lessons as a public speaker: there are no happy endings. Much of your audience will disengage, with a few of them even falling asleep (literally). Most of your audience will remain expressionless, even when you crack the joke you spent the previous day rehearsing. Your evaluations will verify that you were good, maybe even great, but also that you were terrible (and that your shirt was hanging out). You will receive an email asking you about something you never said. Worse, virtually every attendee will leave the room without glancing back. All of this will happen despite your use of every technique outlined in this book. No happy endings indeed.

For nearly thirty minutes, the University of Alberta academics peppered me with questions about, you guessed it, no happy endings. Are all public performances this tragic they asked? I answered with an analogy. Spaghetti westerns are all action: engrossing and provocative. It is a captivating, exciting, and memorable film genre, which is why it never goes away. Yet, they never end well: the protagonist dies; the protagonist's child, parents, or siblings die; even the death of the antagonist pains us as the protagonist rides off into the sunset, broken and alone. Despite the certainty of unhappy endings, we return to the film genre over and over. Our interest is not in how the film ends, but how it unfolds. The same is true for public performances.

You are learning about public speaking because you wish to be better. These techniques combined with practice and commitment will help you improve. Much of your audience will appreciate the new techniques, even if they neither notice nor praise you for them. You will be more confident because you understand the ins and outs of the craft. This is your motivation and your reward. As I told the professors, if you require affirmation from others, you are on the wrong path. You will receive some affirmation, but the condemnations will burn, chafe, and scar you.

Counter-intuitively, I found this realisation empowering. I no longer fret about the rolling eyes or the single-star reviews. I accept that this story does not end well.

YOU WILL HAVE BAD DAYS

Bad days are inevitable. You know this; I know this; and the audience knows this. Knowledge notwithstanding, we fret about these days as though we're being lowered into the ground. We can't avoid bad days. There are too many variables to account for: family, health, hormones, and mood. Since we can't identify the variable, we cannot prevent them. I qualify this claim as some of us face identifiable obstacles, such as illness, poverty, and discrimination, manifestations that instigate bad days galore.

Since we cannot eliminate them, we must learn to handle them. Here we practise the 'best offence is a good defence' approach, developing fallback strategies that we can roll out as needed. Fallback strategies help us out of hot water. For example, when on my bike in the streets of London, I occasionally go through a red light or the wrong way down a road if it means escaping a perilous situation. Doing so on the regular is ill-advised but, infrequently, it is an ace up your sleeve.

What do fallback strategies look like? If you are having a bad day—meaning a poor performance—your aim is not to improve the performance but to glide through it. Get to the end with no major muck-ups. Here are my preferred approaches:

- Speak slowly: speed precipitates anxiety, so by slowing down I catch my breath
- Avoid questions: I signal to the enquirer that I will address their question later (I never do)

- Tell stories: you are the expert of your stories and thus cannot be challenged (they are also naturally captivating, as per my discussion in Chapter 10)
- Disperse: I introduce small-group exercises and probe the groups afterwards, allowing them to shape the performance (and moving the spotlight away from me)
- Recite: if familiar enough with the topic, I recycle a speech I delivered previously, jokes and all (the audience was not there for the original and, even if they were, are unlikely to call you out on it)

You should not be ashamed of having a bad day. There is, however, much shame in knowing that these are inevitable and not developing a strategy to manage them.

THE NEXT PERFORMANCE
WILL BE BETTER

When you have a bad day or, as is often the case, when you think you had a bad day, disappointment and doubt rear their joint head. We berate ourselves for failing to plan, prepare, or practice sufficiently. The disappointment soon morphs into doubt about our abilities as a public speaker. Are we truly cut out for this? Maybe we should retreat and search for a role with less pressure and risk.

Disappointment and doubt are the hobgoblins of sincere minds. Our performance disappointed us for we have high expectations and now question whether we possess the qualities to satisfy audiences over and over. Both are sincere sentiments, which is why I have great sympathy for speakers who suffer their craft. Empathy is easy for I recall succumbing to these same feelings in the past. Now I know better: the next talk will be different.

I will take this assertion to my grave. Bad days chafe a little less. Consider this a cognitive version of muscle memory. For those who do not know, our muscles keep memories of the previous exertions they underwent; they are smart like that. Athletes cycle their training, hence the occasional photo of a fat boxer or footballer that pop up on social media. It is impossible for our bodies to maintain peak performance in much the same way as riding a motorcycle at full throttle will melt your engine. Athletes cycle their training throughout the year, scheduling their peaks during the competition season. They can cycle as their muscles remember the stress we placed them under and can return to their optimal state.

Our minds also have muscle memory, which is why a scent, sound, or smile can cause a Pavlovian recall of the actual feelings. In this very moment, each of us can recollect a scene from our past that will trigger chills, mirth, tears, or even set our nostrils aflare. Our mind remembers. To our great chagrin, the feelings provoked by our memories are not as acute as the ones that happen in real-time. Though I say to those who wish to relive the butterflies of their first love that they should never forget the sheer damnation of that first heartbreak!

The same is true for repeat events: the intensity lessens as time goes on. I suggest the following test to verify my claim. In the coming days, tell a funny story to family or friends. They will laugh and you will feel satisfaction. Wait two days, and retell the same story to another audience. While your narration will elicit a similar reaction, your satisfaction of having made them laugh will not. Since you have already experienced the sensation, the effect is tempered. For you as a comedian or as a romantic this spells doom, but for you as a public speaker this is essential.

To reiterate, despite the optics, public speaking is a thankless gig. You get a lot of attention, but not all attention is desirable, and some of it is hateful and hurtful. You must learn to navigate this feedback in the same way that you learn to navigate the bad days that I spoke about earlier. What I learned from my second court appearance, my second public appearance, and my second university lecture is that the suffering eases. Being berated and judged is not as bad the second time, or the third, and fourth, and so on.

To be clear, awareness will not usher you to the gates of Zen nor will you find peace with yourself and the world. Subsequent talks are easier because you won't suffer as much. It is the suffering that disrupts flow and use of the techniques. Suffering begets anxiety, and anxiety would throw even David Bowie off kilter. In time, you will experience a little less anxiety when audience members yawn. You will maintain your composure and deliver a stronger and more confident performance.

No matter how disappointed you feel after your (supposed) worst performance, know that the likelihood of ever feeling that low again is negligible. Every session expands your experiences and enhances your ability to deal with the unexpected. If you follow the guidance in this book, inevitably, your future performances will improve.

WHAT CHARACTERISES THE IDEAL SPEAKER?

When coaching speakers, I ask them to paint a picture of their ideal speaker. The only condition is detail: they must avoid abstract concepts such as confident or charismatic. Since no one aspires to insecurity or blandness, these characteristics are unhelpful for the exercise. To help inspire genuine reflection, I follow up with questions that many perceive as pedantic and superficial.

- How are they dressed: trousers, skirt, formal, casual, smart, etc.?
- What kind of carrier is in their hand: briefcase, satchel, sleeve? Is it made of leather, canvas, or reclaimed rubber?
- How do they carry themselves in front of the audience? Sober and sophisticated? Chatty and cheerful?
- Do they stand still or do they pace?
- Do they do this on a daily, monthly, or yearly basis? What size and type of audience are they speaking to?

When describing their ideal speaker, they are really describing their ideal self. Each question helps frame their aspiration in concrete terms. The exercise is easier and harder than it seems. It is easier as you paint a picture of someone else. Imagine I asked you to describe your aspirations: its personal nature complicates the query. By imagining another, your anxiety diminishes. However, it is also harder to answer. Our ideal speaker seems light years away from us. We realise that we have a daunting task ahead, or so it seems.

When I first began as a barrister, I read books by courtroom superstars. I sat in galleys and observed them in action. I watched old clips of master orators: Fidel Castro and Malcolm X were two of my favourites. When describing the ideal speaker, I gravitated towards the best qualities of the best speakers. This was a flawed approach. Messi is a phenomenal footballer, Biles is a glorious gymnast, and Williams is a tremendous tennis player, each one being the GOAT in their craft. But that is neither here nor there. When describing my ideal speaker, I should not have imagined perfection. And I am not asking you to either. Our ideal speaker is not a perfect one; rather, it is the one we aspire to be. I admire Biles, Castro, Malcolm, Messi, and Williams, but I do not wish to become them. My aim is to become the ideal me.

This is a key point. I intend nothing in this book to change who you are. One of life's joys is the endless variety of people we encounter. We possess unique qualities, just as we are afflicted with distinct shortcomings. A coach seeks to enhance the qualities an individual possesses and to help them mediate their shortcomings. Even the shortcomings are part of them and can prove charming under the right circumstances.

Once I realised that my goal is to improve 'me', I could run the exercise in a manner that supported my growth as a public speaker. I would not try to be Malcolm X but would instead aspire to my ideal speaker. This person:

- Smiles frequently and widely
- Does not read from materials
- Meanders effortlessly around the room, sometimes nearing a strut
- Can appear a little heavy-handed but committed and sincere
- Dresses sharply and sports eccentric socks
- Carries a sleeve or satchel, both of the hipster variety
- Is an iconoclast spurning conventions and norms at will

I am certain that my ideal speaker is not the ideal speaker of many of the readers of this book. It would be odd if they were! Who I am describing is my ideal speaker and the one I am gradually becoming. I expect many of these features are familiar to my colleagues. When reflecting on the people I train, it occurs to me that none aspire to the strutting or iconoclasm. These are not qualities unique to me, but qualities unique to my speaking style. Admittedly, the eccentric socks have become mundane... damn hipsters.

Do I wish to perfect myself like Messi and Biles? Not in the least. What I wish for, and what I continue to struggle towards, is to achieve the perfection that I am capable of.

*

To reiterate, disappointment precipitated each reflection. Yet, each also proved to be a treasure trove. I learned to accept that public speaking is mostly a thankless affair. But I no longer fret about it. I still have bad days, but I know how to deal with them so my audience is none the wiser. Attendees still leave critical reviews: I should do more of this and less of that. Even days where I am tongue-tied or worn-out do not shake me, for I know that I will be more articulate and lively tomorrow. There may not be any happy endings to public performances, but each one can be a fortunate occurrence if we remain committed and true to the ideal speaker I—and you—aspire to be.

ABOUT THE AUTHOR

Dr. Mohsen al Attar has delivered hundreds of speeches to audiences around the world including the UK, Australia, China, Canada, the US, Kenya, South Africa, Malaysia, and Singapore. He speaks on topics ranging from economic integration to trade wars, from university management to, you guessed it, public speaking.

Mohsen is the Dean of the Faculty of Law at The University of the West Indies and an Associate Professor at the University of Warwick. He is known as a dynamic and in-demand public speaker and lecturer. As a former litigator (barrister), he began honing his speaking skills in courtrooms and boardrooms alike before transferring his craft to the lecture theatre. He actively publishes, podcasts, and speaks on all matters legal, pedagogical, and professional.

ABOUT SPEECH SIMPLIFIED

This book began with a bold claim: people are not afraid of speaking in public. My position runs contrary to popular perception. In fact, going by the descriptor of many books on public speaking, you and others are not just afraid but terrified. I don't agree. Remember Jerry Seinfeld's gag? According to studies, public speaking is our number one fear. Number two is death. But consider the context. Ask anyone to do something they have never done before a) in public, b) with an audience judging your performance, and c) while keeping them captivated. Who subjects themselves to this level of hell? Why do they believe they would be good at it?

Yet, we expect this for public speaking. Because we can 'speak', we presume we can do so under any circumstances. To use a silly metaphor: how many of us would stand up in front of an audience and passionately kiss someone for an hour under the gaze of a crowd? I feel my anxiety rise just writing about this.

If you accept my premise—and, if you made it this far, I presume that you do—then you also accept my solution: practise the techniques outlined in this book. It is not rocket science. You are learning to tell a story in a structured manner to captivate your audience and be remembered. It may not be everyone's cup of tea but, unlike chess, mathematics, or tennis—all activities that require a lot of practice before you can manage even the basics—anyone can learn to speak in public with high skill. This results from the logic and simplicity of the techniques I develop in this book.

*

Practice is essential and, on my website, I provide a series of training regimes for anyone eager to take their learning to a higher level. Another option is the webinars, workshops, and coaching I provide, and I dedicate the rest of this section to telling you briefly about the services we offer at Speech Simplified. To be clear, I am confident that anyone can achieve proficiency by practising the techniques outlined in this book. I would not have written it, nor would I be promoting it if I did not believe this to be the case. You can take this book and the training regimes and get cracking on your own. This is an effective approach. A better way is to organise a group and practice with others since, as you may have noticed, you must perform these techniques in front of an audience.

Another pathway that some readers opt for is to enrol in one of Speech Simplified's offerings. These, too, can be effective in helping you enhance your abilities in public speaking. Reading a book is a passive action. You gain information, yes, but you are not developing the skills, hence why you must practise. Whether you pursue this on your own, in a group, or with me, it is essential that you move your learning from passive to active.

Options differ and only some are suitable for you. My webinars explain some techniques of public speaking and, best of all, provide a live example of the techniques. I offer several of these throughout the year and on a range of topics. Most are free, and others command a minor fee. Workshops are more nuanced. With the luxury of time and partners, the training is interactive. Individuals can make immense gains through the workshops as the small size ensures that both lessons and exercises cohere, providing a wide exposure to techniques and supportive examples. More important than the exposure, however, is the practice. You will watch me deliver these techniques, but you will also watch others and showcase yourself during the workshop. Being more interactive, those who prefer workshops wish to develop their abilities alongside others.

Last, I welcome those who wish to receive personalised training, whether individually or in a group. There is no set type of person who signs up. Many of my clients are lawyers who wish to develop specific advocacy skills. As Keith Evans observed, every barrister benefits from advocacy training, yet few pursue it. I have also coached professors who wish to make their lectures or their conference presentations more engaging. Since many academics rely on the scripted speech, this training can take multiple forms; learning to write and recite a captivating and memorable presentation or, and this is what I encourage, learning to relinquish the crutch and deliver a riveting performance with minimal notes.

Most of all, my coaching is popular among a range of professionals, from early career to senior management. Like the world of law, the world of business (in for-profit and not-for-profit sectors) demands efficiency, hence the interest of these individuals in acquiring efficient public speaking skills. Unlike the world of law, however, the world of business also demands pizzazz. As directors, executives, and managers know all too well, a fair share of business depends on first impressions. The ability to rock the mic conveys the gravitas that inspires confidence and closes deals. Since these constituencies work and travel in packs, they often request small group coaching or bespoke workshops, which I design and deliver.

*

Learning is freedom. I will also take this claim to the grave. I have not felt more or less free in one country or another, one relationship or another, with greater or lesser wealth. My freedom comes from knowledge and from the act of learning.

Learning something new is empowering. We understand more of the world and of ourselves. This creates opportunities to pursue pathways more suited to our aspirations or to reorient ourselves away from pathways we have exhausted. In short, we get closer to our ideal self, whoever that is. I hope this book helps you along your path, or causes you to shift onto another, more fitting one. If you would like additional guidance, Speech Simplified might be for you. Even if you do not, get in touch anyway: I enjoy hearing from everyone who has read the book whether they wish to praise me for it or, since there are no happy endings, berate me for it. You are most welcome regardless.

Maybe I am romanticising self-actualisation. I'm probably over-emphasising the link between learning and life. Perhaps. I look forward to your captivating and memorable speech about why that is.